HOPE
IN TIMES OF
CRISIS

GUILLERMO MALDONADO

HOPE
IN TIMES OF
CRISIS

Our Vision

To fill the Earth with the knowledge of God's glory.

————————

"I have called you to bring
My supernatural power to this generation

Hope in Times of Crisis

978-1-59272-330-0
Edition October 2009
This publication may not be reproduced or transmitted in any form or any means, archived in electronic system nor transmitted in any electronic, mechanical, including photocopying, recording, or by any information storage retrieval system, or any other manner, without the previous written permission of the author.

Unless otherwise indicated, all Scripture quotations are taken from the New King James Version of the Bible. Scripture quotations taken from THE AMP, Copyright © 1954, 1958, 1962, 1965, 1987 by the Lockman Foundation. All rights reserved. Used by permission. www.Lockman.org)

Cover Design by:
ERJ Publicaciones

Translated by:
Jackie Delgado and Henrry Becerra

Published by:
ERJ Publicaciones
13651 SW 143 Ct., Suite 101, Miami, FL 33186
Tel: (305) 233-3325 - Fax: (305) 675-5770

Category:
Spiritual Growth

Printed in the USA

I wish to express my sincere gratitude to God's children, the faithful and radical who believe in His promises and know who their God is. I am eternally thankful to the King Jesus congregation and to my spiritual children, in the United States and the rest of the world, for in times of crisis you have prayed and stood firm and strong. Thank you for your faithfulness and your ministerial and financial support. God bless you!

INDEX
 convolution

C risis is a term that greatly emphasizes the possibility of change, and it is marked by a new order of things. By nature, human beings resist change and tend to have a great deal of difficulty letting go of any situation under our control. Adapting ourselves to new situations may cause us stress, discomfort, and uncertainty. For that reason, crisis carries a negative connotation, one I challenge you to change. This book is directed towards *everyone*, Christian or not: teachers, politicians, businessmen, employers, professionals, doctors, engineers, students, or housewives.

Though you might have a hard time accepting it, my theory is that crisis is actually a great opportunity for change and progress. The secret is to learn to ride the waves of this world without wiping out. Surfers wait for the perfect wave. Their goal is to stay on the surfboard the greatest possible amount of time. The more experienced surfers might do fancy tricks while riding the gigantic waves, and when the wave dies down, they get off their boards with elegance and begin the process all over again. The beginners often stumble and fall in the violent thrashing formed by the water, sand, and rocks. In fact, many suffer severe injuries; the same happens in our lives. We are often defeated because of our inability to ride the waves of thrashing circumstances present in our lives. The question we must ask ourselves now is, "What will we do in the face of adversity? Do we learn how to skillfully ride the waves or do we allow ourselves to be wiped out?"

Albert Einstein mentioned something about crisis, and it went along these lines:

"Let us not pretend that things are going to change if we continue to do the same thing. Crisis is the best blessing that can happen to people and countries because it brings progress. Creativity is born from anxiety, just as day is birthed from the dark night. It is in crisis that discoveries, inventions, and great strategies are born. Whoever surpasses crisis surpasses self, and whoever blames crisis for their shames and failures rejects their own talents while respecting problems more than its solutions. The true crisis is the crisis of incompetence, and the real problem that people and countries face is their laziness to find ways to deal with a crisis and its possible solutions. Without crisis times there are no challenges, and without challenges life becomes a routine, a slow agony to bear. There is no merit without crisis. It is during crisis times that the best of each of us comes out. To speak about a crisis is to promote it, and to be quiet in crisis is to exalt conformity, so instead of promoting it or conforming to it, let us deal with the true crisis once and for all—the tragedy of not wanting to fight to overcome."

Whatever your crisis might be—financial, physical, emotional, matrimonial, or anything related to work, your existence, family, identity, values or beliefs—you should know there is a solution. Hope is the anchor that keeps your boat steady in the midst of a storm and the key to your decision-making and success. We were created with the ability to overcome every test and adversity, but to successfully do this, we need to set aside all feeling of anxiety and desperation and take bold action.

In my life, I have personally dealt with many difficult crises times, of all shapes and sizes. In this book, I briefly share how I was educated to have a pessimistic outlook on life and what it took for me to change it. I have experienced many challenges that have stretched my faith and expanded my mentality. Today, I still face crises and challenges, but rather than feeling sorry for myself, I welcome them knowing the potential of growth and progress they can mean in my life. The text you are about to read is full of personal experiences designed to teach you how to see things from a different perspective, as well as to give you the tools that will make you an expert in dealing with your own crisis. The basis of my advice is strictly founded in biblical principles, inspired by God and which revolve around Jesus being the Cornerstone— the unshakeable Rock, and anyone who grabs hold of Him will survive any storm and succeed.

CHAPTER I

৵৵৵

Who Has the Answers
in Times of Crisis
and for the Future?

৵৵৵

Without a doubt, we are living in times of crisis. These are difficult moments. Throughout the world, there are people who feel uneasy, insecure, anxious, and fearful due to the many things that are happening today, in particular, in the area of worldwide financial instability. People, both within and outside of the Church, have questions that need to be answered. Who has those answers? Who can tell them what will happen in the next five or ten years? The Bible, God's inspired word, has the following to say regarding this matter.

"¹To everything there is a season, a time for every purpose under heaven: ²a time to be born, and a time to die; a time to plant, and a time to pluck what is planted; ³a time to kill, and a time to heal; a time to break down, and a time to build up; ⁴a time to weep, and a time to laugh; a time to mourn, and a time to dance; ⁵a time to cast away stones, and a time to gather stones; a time to embrace, and a time to refrain from embracing; ⁶a time to gain, and a time to lose; a time to keep, and a time to throw away; ⁷a time to tear, and a time to sew; a time to keep silence, and a time to speak; ⁸a time to love, and a time to hate; a time of war, and a time of peace." Ecclesiastes 3:1-8

Due to the great wisdom God gave Solomon, one of the two greatest kings of Israel, we see in these verses fourteen instances in life for which there is an appointed time.

The opposite of each instance is noted to show that there is a time for each to take place. An important point to understand is that we will inevitably have to experience those instances which are part of life. Jesus took it further and spoke to us about *knowing* the times in which we live.

"¹Then the Pharisees and Sadducees came, and testing Him asked that He would show them a sign from heaven. ²He answered and said to them, 'When it is evening you say, 'It will be fair weather, for the sky is red'; ³and in the morning, 'It will be foul weather today, for the sky is red and threatening.' Hypocrites! You know how to discern the face of the sky, but you cannot discern the signs of the times!'" Matthew 16:1-3

Unfortunately, the generation that lived during Jesus' time on earth did not recognize or discern the time of His coming; and so, many rejected, condemned, and ultimately crucified Him. Why? It was because they did not discern the times! Jesus told the Pharisees that they knew how to discern the signs of nature but not those of spiritual times; the same is happening today. We recognize natural seasons like summer, fall, winter, and spring, but we fail to discern the *spiritual times* we live in.

"¹But concerning the times and the seasons, brethren, you have no need that I should write to you. ²For you yourselves know perfectly that the day of the Lord so comes as a thief in the night." 1 Thessalonians 5:1, 2

Paul said we are children of light, and that as such, we should know the times in which we live. What time are we in today? That is the question we must ask ourselves. The answer is that we are going through a time in which the Earth is being judged due to different causes that will be mentioned later. Everything everywhere is being shaken; hence, the importance to understand this season in order to have a sense of direction for our life, future, and children but, more importantly, to learn what to do in times of crisis.

🐦🐦🐦

Success in life depends on doing
the right thing at the right time.

🐦🐦🐦

It is not always the right time to plant or the right time to pluck. It is not always the right time to seek or the right time to lose. It is not always the right time to destroy or to build up. It is not always the right time to speak just as it is not always correct to be silent; but there is, however, a time to cry and a time to laugh.

How do we know when the time is right for each thing? The answer to that question will determine if we succeed or fail in life; it is crucial. That is why the Scriptures teach us that time is a mystery.

Through which two agents will God reveal the future or upcoming events to us?

1. The Holy Spirit

"[13]However, when He, the Spirit of truth, has come, He will guide you into all truth; for He will not speak on His own

authority, but whatever He hears He will speak; and He will tell you things to come." John 16:13

Time may be a mystery to scientists, but not for the Holy Spirit, for He is the only One who can show us what to do, when, and in which season. Why do I so confident in saying this? It is because He hears the Father and knows His plans. The Holy Spirit knows the innermost secret things of God. It is from there that stems the affirmation that we are not able to do anything without Him. Since the emergence of civilized society, mankind has sought to de-vise a system that could function without the Holy Spirit, but it has been unable thus far to develop one that is free of ills and violence. Many try to impose rules, systems, and structures that seem good and mean well but that ultimately does not work.

Example: Discipleship is one of the commandments of the Great Commission, [1] established by Jesus. However, if we establish it as a system of rules and traditions, it will become like any other religious method. Without the direction of the Holy Spirit, it will not work. In Christian living, nothing works without the Holy Spirit's guidance. When we try to do good things for God, in our own strength and as we see fit, He will forgive us but will never prosper us. The Father and the Son jealously guard the Holy Spirit's reputation and see to it that we give Him His due place in the Church as

---

[1] Matthew 28.19 and Mark 16.15. Discipleship is the strategy created to train and equip disciples to live and preach the Good News of Jesus Christ and to disciple others; this system is similar to the one used by the business world in their use of mentors to train potential business leaders.

God and Lord. He is the only person that will let us know what will happen in the future and cause us to understand what is happening in the present. When we go to the Scriptures, we see that the Holy Spirit never speaks of Himself or for Himself. If you want to be a friend of the Father and of the Son, you need to also be a friend of the Holy Spirit, and give Him the place in your life He ought to have. Jesus sent Him to be our Comforter and Counselor; to reveal the Father and show us all things.

ॐॐॐ
*The Holy Spirit is the administrator
of the riches of the Kingdom of God.*
ॐॐॐ

We are heirs in Christ, but the administrator of that inheritance is the Holy Spirit. The prophet Zachariah confirms this:

"⁶So he answered and said to me: 'this is the word of the LORD to Zerubbabel: 'Not by might nor by power, but by My Spirit,' says the LORD of hosts.'" Zachariah 4.6

This principle is related with what we read in Ecclesiastes. God will not do anything in human strength or wisdom. He will not use armies of men, swords, horses, arsenals, missiles, or anything created by man. Whatever God decides to do will be done with the power of the Holy Spirit.

2. The written Word of God

The other agent of God to reveal the times and the future to us is His Word. Throughout history, man has always desired to know or predict the future. He has sought methods and ways to discover it through reason, the senses, emotions, and mysticism. Man has employed methods dating back thousands of years such as astrology, sorcery, witchcraft, palmistry, tarot card readings, and other forms of mysticism. The Bible stresses that when man sought to know the future in that manner, the findings were incorrect and deceitful and resulted in evil befalling the people. In recent days, mankind has sought more sophisticated ways of knowing the future, mostly through scientific methods, opinion polls, surveys, prospectuses, scenarios, and the training of experts in areas such as physics, financial planning, economics, and others. With the aid of technology, computers, and applied science, mankind has found ways to predict or foresee the future, achieving its greatest success, to that end, in the field of climate forecasting. Though advancement is evident, mankind has not found definitive answers because no human being is able to predict the future with absolute scientific certainty. None of those investigations are without a margin of error and thus are not completely reliable. Therefore, I base my assertion that there is only one truly reliable source that knows the times and that is the Word of God. It tells us what He knows about the future.

Why is the Word of God trustworthy?

+ **The Bible sheds light on the future.**

"¹⁰⁵Your word is a lamp to my feet and a light to my path." Psalms 119:105

If you delve into the Word, it will illuminate your future and your life. It will teach you to do the right thing in times of crisis and difficulty.

•   **God declares in the Bible that He will predict the future.**

"⁶Thus says the LORD, the King of Israel, and his Redeemer, the LORD of hosts: 'I am the First and I am the Last; besides Me there is no God. ⁷And who can proclaim as I do? Then let him declare it and set it in order for Me, since I appointed the ancient people. And the things that are coming and shall come, let them show these to them. ⁸Do not fear, nor be afraid; have I not told you from that time, and declared it? You are My witnesses. Is there a God besides Me? Indeed there is no other Rock; I know not one." Isaiah 44:6-8

The Lord says: "I am God, the only true God, maker of the heavens and the Earth. I am the First and the Last, the Alpha and Omega. I know what happened in the past and what will happen in the future because I was the One who created time." He adds, "If anyone wants to challenge Me as God, show up with your knowledge of the future like I have it. Only I possess that knowledge, and I grant it to those that seek Me with their hearts."

The God that Proclaims the Future Guides us Through the Present.

"⁹Remember the former things of old, for I am God, and there is no other; I am God, and there is none like Me, ¹⁰declaring the end from the beginning, and from ancient times things that are not yet done, saying, 'My counsel shall stand, and I will do all My pleasure.'" Isaiah 46:9, 10

God says, "I know the beginning. My purpose shall remain, and I will do whatever I want to do." For this reason, it is important to join God's purpose because His is the only one that will withstand the test of time in a world where everything has been shaken and where no one is trustworthy! Only God's Word, His purpose, and His will are truly reliable.

What is God's reaction against other sources that predict the future?

"²⁴Thus says the LORD, your Redeemer, and He who formed you from the womb: 'I am the LORD, who makes all things, who stretches out the heavens all alone, who spreads abroad the earth by Myself; ²⁵who frustrates the signs of the babblers, and drives diviners mad; who turns wise men backward, and makes their knowledge foolishness; ²⁶who confirms the word of His servant, and performs the counsel of His messengers; who says to Jerusalem, 'You shall be inhabited,' to the cities of Judah, 'You shall be built,' and I will raise up her waste places.'" Isaiah 44:24-26

Here is the contrast between the fortunetellers and godly men. God confirms the word of His servants—the apostles and prophets—and performs their counsel. When someone independent of God predicts the future, He frustrates their signs and confuses their predictions. In the end, only God's Word will remain and the prophecies of the apostles and prophets that He chose as His mouthpiece to reveal the future to His people. God Himself essentially said, "I made the heavens and the Earth. I know what will happen in the future, and I know how to guide you into and through that future. I am in complete control." I maintain that the Bible is the only reliable source that has stood on its own merit throughout history. What do I base that on?

- **The Bible has a proven record of perfect accuracy**

  Every prophecy written about Jesus was fulfilled in His life exactly as they were told. We see the same take place regarding the destiny of Israel, from its inception to this day. Everything the Bible states about this nation has come to pass.

- **The Bible predicts the future with authority, precision, and accuracy**

  Therefore, we should trust in it as well as in the Holy Spirit, or Spirit of Truth, who guides and shows us the future. This should give us the confidence we need in an insecure world, especially during crisis times. At all times, the Word of God will be the anchor to which we can cling to and feel safe with, knowing that our God is in control and will guide us to a safe harbor.

Which human instruments will God use to predict the future on Earth?

The human instruments God uses to predict future events on Earth are the apostles and prophets. He chooses them, assigns them a purpose, and then backs them up in that assignment.

"¹Now the angel who talked with me came back and wakened me, as a man who is wakened out of his sleep. ²And he said to me, 'What do you see?' So I said, 'I am looking, and there is a lampstand of solid gold with a bowl on top of it, and on the stand seven lamps with seven pipes to the seven lamps. ³Two olive trees are by it, one at the right of the bowl and the other at its left.' ¹⁴So he said, 'These are the two anointed ones, who stand beside the Lord of the whole earth.'" Zachariah 4:1-3,14

In these verses, the Holy Spirit speaks to us about the ministry of the apostle and the prophet. They have been assigned to answer the questions being asked by the world and the Church; questions such as: Is it time to build? Is it time to sow? Is it time to dance? Is it time to plant? Is it time for judgment? Is it time for war? Is it time for peace? God uses both of these ministries, represented by the olive trees on both sides of the lampstand, to provide the Church with fresh oil and to tell it what to do. One grave problem of the Church today is that it is living on old oil; this was never God's intention for the Church, for old wine does not work in new times.

God is currently moving throughout the world. That which was new five years ago is obsolete, old, or outdated today.

Sadly, most people continue to do the same thing they did five years ago, not knowing they are out of God's timing.

The Holy Spirit raised or restored the ministry of the apostle and the prophet to bring new wine to old wineskins, to pour new oil into the lamps, and to feed His Church. Many people became successful years ago using something that brought forth life at the time. However, rather than trying to reuse their methods or mentality, we should prepare ourselves for what God is doing today; otherwise, we will be outside of God's timing and will fail to walk or do the right things. The previous Bible text mentions two olive trees; these symbolize two men that will come in the future whose ministries will be restored on Earth—Moses and Elijah. Moses represents the ministry of the apostle while Elijah represents the prophet.

"³And I will give power to my two witnesses, and they will prophesy one thousand two hundred and sixty days, clothed in sackcloth. ⁴These are the two olive trees and the two lampstands standing before the God of the earth." Revelations 11:3, 4

Fresh oil springs from the olive trees and travels to the lampstand via two pipes; thus, providing bright light. If the oil supply is interrupted, the light radiated by the lampstand is extinguished—the oil represents the Holy Spirit of God.

Everyone needs answers to their questions; their quest comes from the fact that they don't have light. They do not have a vision of what is happening in the present or what is to occur in the future. That is why there must be a constant supply of fresh oil. We cannot function without fresh, clean oil; without the inspiration and revelation of the Holy Spirit which comes from the apostolic and prophetic ministries. We all need to be continually nourished; therefore, we need to recognize and accept both of these ministries in order to receive the fresh oil needed for crisis times and to illuminate what God wants to give in the present and in the future.

"18Where there is no revelation, the people cast off restraint; but happy is he who keeps the law." Proverbs 29:18

Another translation reads, "Where there is no vision, or a fresh and direct revelation from God, the people become unbridled." The world, including many churches and ministries, currently practice a religion. What is religion? It is traditions, rites, practices, and customary rules that are not conducive to a personal and intimate relationship with God. Religion is not enough to sustain the Church and to light the world. From the lampstand must flow the fresh oil that comes from the Holy Spirit. It is not a matter of just reading and teaching the Bible, but rather, of having an immediate, fresh, *Rhema* of God. It is a matter of having supernatural revelation of God's knowledge to discern the times we are living in, what awaits us in the future, and what we should do in times of crisis.

Doctrinal or biblical teaching alone never substitutes fresh and direct revelation received firsthand from God. We are not referring to a general teaching, but rather, to a specific and refreshing revelation, a vision or prophecy for this particular and difficult time which warns us of future events. In the days when Eli served as the priest in the Tabernacle, there was no vision. That is why God brought Samuel who represents the prophetic and later David that personifies the apostolic.

"¹Now the boy Samuel ministered to the LORD before Eli. And the word of the LORD was rare in those days; there was no widespread revelation." 1 Samuel 3:1

What happens when there is a lack of vision or a fresh revelation from God?

Due to a lack of the presence of God and of a fresh revelation of His will, the people moved away from Him. They lived in darkness because oil was scarce and there was nothing to replenish the lamps with. That is the same thing that happens today. People go about without direction, without guidance. They separate from the church. The people are lost and do not know what to do. The same happens all over the world. People want answers, and those answers are held by the Holy Spirit and the Word of God.

The Holy Spirit is using both of these ministries, the apostolic and the prophetic, to supply oil to the Church and to give light to the world. The light allows the world and the Church to see and hear what God is doing today, what is happening at this critical moment, and how to make it through any crisis.

I have pointed out that this is a time of a global shaking. The international economy has suffered a historical, unprecedented, incalculable imbalance. Can today's apostles and prophets say why this has occurred? Can they explain the cause? Can they give the world answers so we can know what to do? Of course they can! Long ago, God said through the apostles and prophets that He would shake up the global economy, particularly the economy of the United States of America, as it would put riches and greed before God. In other words, the people have replaced God with another god, the dollar bill. Therefore, God has allowed the purchasing power of the dollar to be devalued, in such a way, that He is essentially saying to the American people, "I devalue the power of your god." Let us then change our mentality and deposit our trust in God and in His kingdom which shall never be moved.

~~~

God uses the apostle and the prophet
to give His people direction and
to bring fresh revelation.

~~~

The Nineveh prophecy came because God wanted its inhabitants to know that judgment was close at hand. Another time He wanted the people of Israel to know that the Messiah would come and at yet another time He wanted Paul to know what awaited him in Jerusalem. All of this could not have come from a general revelation of the Scriptures. Within the Church, the ministries of the pastor, the evangelist, and the teacher are entrusted with teaching doctrine, both general aspects as well as specific topics of the Bible, including: history, context, application, etc. However, it is the apostles and prophets that the Holy Spirit uses to provide prompt direction to His people for specific times and to bring fresh revelation from the heavens to the Earth.

We live in times of great peril and depression. There are voices today affirming that they predicted with precision the magnitude of the current economic crisis, but that is not sustainable. Even though there were predictions, without exception they all fell short. Why? It is because no human mind is able to conceive, without a margin of error, what will happen in society, the economy, or in military or international relations during the next five years.

If there were ever a time in which the people of God need a fresh revelation, a vision of the Father, it is now. There are circumstances that we cannot understand through natural sources of information but only through the revelation of the Holy Spirit, as spoken through His servants, the apostles and the prophets.

"⁷By faith Noah, being divinely warned of things not yet seen, moved with godly fear, prepared an ark for the saving of his household, by which he condemned the world and became heir of the righteousness which is according to faith." Hebrews 11:7

Noah needed a divine revelation to warn him that rain would come. God gave specific instructions, particularly to him and to his family, regarding what steps they should take. Just like Noah, lately I have become persuaded that we are to remain open to specific and direct revelation from God, a message that given its punctuality cannot come just through the regular teaching of the Bible nor by natural means. If Christianity is to shine in this time of darkness, it is necessary for the ministries of the apostle and of the prophet to provide oil to the lampstand.

To function in the ministry of the apostle and of the prophet is not just about saying, "Thus says the Lord..."; it also includes supplying the fresh oil that Christians and the people need as they seek God. The apostles and the prophets reveal the mysteries of God hidden in His word.

What are the mysteries of the Bible?

*   The revealed things: which belong to the Church
*   The secret things: that belong to God

"29The secret things belong to the LORD our God, but those things which are revealed belong to us and to our children forever, that we may do all the words of this law." Deuteronomy 29:29

God's Word teaches that the revealed things are for the children, but the secret things belong only to God. Most believers are busy seeking out the secret things, but have failed to obey the revealed things that God has commanded them to do. If the secret things belong to God, then we should ask *Him* to reveal them to us but only if we have obeyed the revealed things.

We must accept that as mere humans, and as such we have limitations as to what we can do—God does not.

*   **There are questions in life that we will never be able to answer.**

- **There are situations in life that we will never be able to explain.**

  If you want answers or explanations for everything, you will eventually substitute reason for faith.

- **There are things in life that we will never be able to change.**

  Nothing changes by worrying or being anxious over them. We cannot change our past, parents, race, sex, nationality, or the body we were born into. If we tried doing this, we would probably end up depressed because we would be swimming against the tide.

- **There are issues in life we cannot control.**

  If you have reared your child well, counseled him, given him a good example, have taught him the Word, and you have been a good father or a good mother, yet he decides to do wrong, you will not be able to control or restrain him. What is the only thing you can do? Pray!

  When the doctor tells you that you have a terminal illness that is beyond your control neither money, fame, position, nor prestige can control or reverse that adverse situation. Therefore, let us have peace knowing that God is the only one that does have control and the power to change that situation in your favor.

- **There are events in life that cannot be stopped.**

We cannot stop the seasons of a year. There will be spring, summer, fall, and winter. The first verse at the beginning of this book insists on this very thing. There is a time to sow and a time to reap. We cannot change those times and seasons; therefore, let them be so that they do not destroy us, and in the meanwhile, let us rejoice and praise God.

* **There are things for which you are responsible and there are others for which you are not.**

Know where your responsibility ends. You are not responsible for your children's behavior if you have taught them good morals, good conduct, and God's Word. You are only responsible for the decisions you make.

෩෧෩

*You are not responsible for what is
beyond your control and dominion.*

෩෧෩

* **There are limits in life we cannot surpass.**

There will always be someone who is better equipped and who can do things better than we can; this is impossible to change despite how hard we try. In any case, the best thing is to do everything with excellence and to feel satisfied for having put up a good fight.

How do you face life with these limitations?

"[9]...*He said to me, 'My grace is sufficient for you, for My strength is made perfect in weakness.' Therefore most gladly I will rather boast in my infirmities, that the power of Christ may rest upon me." 2 Corinthians 12:9*

We need to accept our limitations and depend completely on the supernatural grace of the Holy Spirit. Remember that the revealed things are for us and that the secret things belong to God. We have access to the secret things if we ask God to reveal them to us, but if He does not want to do so, let us remember the principles that we just learned. In the process, we should have peace and not become anxious or desperate. If we lost our house, our property, or a loved one, we cannot become anxious when we lack answers or an explanation. There are things we will never be able to explain. For example, we cannot explain why we lost a job, got a divorce, why something happened in the past, or why we were abused or rejected as children. In such cases, we should trust God and pray for peace because He will reveal the answers at the appropriate time. In His time, the Holy Spirit will reveal His will to us, but while He reveals it, let us obey and be faithful.

What is the main principle we should understand in times of crisis?

"¹⁰Be still, and know that I am God; I will be exalted among the nations, I will be exalted in the earth." Psalms 46:10

The main principle we should understand in critical times is to let God be God. One of the major problems of the general population, including Christians, is that they try to become god-like, but remember that there are things that only He can do. Men who try to do what only God can do, do so in vain. We are called to do what is possible but God is called to do the impossible. Do not forget that we are mere human beings incapable of doing the impossible. We cannot live on earth without God. Jesus said. "Without me, you can do nothing." Therefore, we should live close to God, in complete dependence of Him, to have victory and bear fruit.

Why do we need to let God be God?

* **There are things that only God knows.**

  We don't know what God knows; therefore, we should obey the One that knows it all and not worry about what we don't know.

* **There are things that only God can understand.**

  People are always trying to understand God, why difficult moments come, and why some things take place. But God cannot be understood because our mind is too finite to do so. We can, however, believe God, but sadly, our faith is often destroyed by the guillotine of reason. God does not command us to understand Him. If you are wondering if God knows what you are going through, let me clear it up for you. He does! He knows about the family member you lost, about your failed marriage, and about the issues you don't understand. He knows more than you and me. Therefore, the only thing you need to know and do is to trust His wisdom, having the certainty that ultimately all things will work out favorably for those that love Him.

♦ **There are things that only God can explain.**

We cannot expect to know or explain why things happen. Sometimes, all we can do is say, "I don't know."

Can a human being with a finite mind argue or question God?

In my ministerial life, I have learned not to question God but rather to simply listen and obey what He tells me. Why? Well, because I have understood and accepted that He knows things that I will never discover on my own. God knows the future and I don't. That is why I don't question Him. When there are things in the ministry that I do not understand, I simply praise Him and give Him thanks. Are you experiencing difficult times that you do not understand? Are you going through a crisis for which there is no apparent explanation? Then simply lift up your hands and praise God.

In summary, we can say that:

♦ We are living in crisis times during which most people feel insecure, fearful, and anxious due to the instability of the economy, of society, etc.

♦ The world seeks answers, and Christians need for God and the Holy Spirit to provide them.

♦ There is a season for all things to take place under heaven. The important thing is to know how to recognize what time we are living in.

* Success in life depends on doing the right thing at the right time.

* The Holy Spirit and the Bible are the two agents God uses to reveal the future to us. The human instruments He uses are apostles and prophets.

* God supports His servants but confuses the fortune-tellers and frustrates the signs of the seers.

* The mysteries found in the Bible consist of the reveled things that belong to the Church and the secret things that belong to God.

* There are questions we will never be able to answer, situations we will never be able to explain, things we will never be able to change, matters we will not be not be able to control, events we will never be able to stop, limits we will not be able to surpass, and responsibilities we should not assume. However, there is one thing we can always be certain of: God is always in control and all things work together for good for those that love Him.

In conclusion, where can we go to find the answers to the questions about the present and the future? There are two venues of information: the Holy Spirit who reveals all things present and future and the Word of God. The Holy Spirit uses human instruments to predict the future, provide answers, guide us, reveal the things of God to the Church and to the world, and to keep us from living in darkness. Apostles and prophets are God's chosen servants, and we should acknowledge and welcome them. The Church and the people that choose not to acknowledge these ministries will live in darkness because without them, there is no way for God's oil to come.

We learned that the secret things belong to God and the reveled ones are for us—we cannot ask God to reveal secret things if we have chosen not to obey Him in regards to the revealed things. If we don't have the answers, if we can't explain, change, or control things, let us simply have peace in our heart and understand that God is in control. If you are experiencing difficult times, then you need to believe that God is in control. Simply say, "Lord, give me Your peace. I don't know how to explain it, it is very difficult to understand, but right now I thank you and give you the glory." We are living in the last days, in crisis times, and God is the only One that knows the past, present, and future—He wants to give us the strength and peace to overcome and succeed. God's judgment is upon the Earth, shaking the world economy, society, values, etc., due to the rampant corruption and degradation of human character as well as mental and sexual corruption. Corruption and violence, as well as the total corruption of society, are topics that will be covered in the following chapter.

CHAPTER II

❧❧❧

Causes and Signs
of the End Times

❧❧❧

M any wonder what the world will be like when the end times draw near. The Word of God contains several significative events regarding the end times that make them different from any other time in the history of humanity. The figure I will present to you, of what is happening in the world, will allow you to confirm for yourself the times we are facing, keeping in mind what you have seen and experienced in your own life. To know what those signs are, we will see what Jesus said when He was on Earth. Likewise, as we study these end times, we will see the cause of what is happening and why we are living in times of crisis. If we understand the cause, we can then cut the root and change our way of living; moreover, we will be able to help others do the same. However, if we lack understanding of the root of the problems, finding a solution will be very difficult.

Presently, rulers and people in positions of authority are seeking solutions for humanity, but they cannot find them. Throughout His Word, Jesus taught us to lift our eyes and know the times that we are living in to provide solutions and guidance to those that walk in darkness.

"26And as it was in the days of Noah, so it will be also in the days of the Son of Man: 27They ate, they drank, they married wives, they were given in marriage, until the day that Noah entered the ark, and the flood came and destroyed them all." Luke 17:26, 27

Jesus compares the days prior to His return to the days of Noah. How were the days of Noah? We will now see these signs which are also the reason the Earth was so corrupted and society was so depraved.

1. The penetration and intense pressure of the occult in humanity.

"¹Now it came to pass, when men began to multiply on the face of the earth, and daughters were born to them, ²that the sons of God saw the daughters of men, that they were beautiful; and they took wives for themselves of all whom they chose." Genesis 6:1, 2

Here we see a reference to individuals called giants which were fallen angels that had sexual relationships with the daughters of men. They were spiritual beings that crossed the barriers of their world to have sexual relationships with human women; thus, entering the physical realm.

"³And the LORD said, 'My Spirit shall not strive with man forever, for he is indeed flesh; yet his days shall be one hundred and twenty years.'" Genesis 6:3

When God saw this, He shortened the life span of humans to 120 years because of the unnatural sexual relationship taking place between spiritual beings and human beings.

"⁴There were giants on the earth in those days, and also afterward, when the sons of God came in to the daughters of men

and they bore children to them. Those were the mighty men who were of old, men of renown." Genesis 6:4

The Hebrew word used here for *giant* is *nephilim*, and it means *the fallen*. This plainly indicates that fallen angels inhabited the Earth in those days and started to have sex with women. This clearly shows the penetration and intense pressure of the occult in society, culture, and the world in the times of Noah.

2. The universal corruption of the human mind.

"⁵Then the LORD saw that the wickedness of man was great in the earth, and that every intent of the thoughts of his heart was only evil continually." Genesis 6:5

The human mind, imaginations, thoughts, intentions, and visions, became contaminated and filthy, and it continues to this day. A police officer and member of our church told me about a man that was arrested for sexually abusing his two-year-old daughter. His own daughter! During his confession, he said, "Well, that's what women are for, to have sex with them." Only a corrupt mind could think that way. This confirms that we are living in days like those of Noah. Humanity's mind becomes more and more corrupt each day.

3. The Earth became corrupt and full of violence.

"¹¹The earth also was corrupt before God, and the earth was filled with violence." Genesis 6:11

Violence was present in all they did, in their actions and conduct. It was normal for the people in Noah's time to act violently. Again, the same is happening today. One day, as I watched a television show, I saw on the news that an eight-year-old child took a gun and killed his parents. After such an atrocity, the boy did not show any remorse. He said that he simply felt the desire to kill them, so he did it.

Right now, the Earth is under a curse caused by violence and murders leading to bloodshed. Those who have been offended enact revenge and hurl curses against their aggressors and retaliate; thus, imposing curses of poverty, sickness, and sterility upon its inhabitants. Only the blood of Jesus' can deal with these curses, for it speaks far better things than Abel's innocent blood—though the innocent blood cries out to God for judgment and vengeance, as His people, we should pray for the blood of Jesus to cry out for mercy and redemption.

Violence is everywhere: in television shows, cartoons, movies, children's programming, the news, and more. The Earth is full of violence, wars, murders, destruction, death, and more, as in the days of Noah.

4. Corruption and sexual perversion

"12...God looked upon the earth, and indeed it was corrupt; for all flesh had corrupted their way on the earth."Genesis 6:12

We have seen an increase in homosexual groups and activities. In order to establish their moral and sexual corruption, they demand their rights and try to impose their behavior everywhere: in schools, literature, films, churches, nations, governments, and more. Even when it seems like they have gone too far, perhaps you are not taking into account their desire to impose themselves in a "peaceful" manner but also through violence and aggression.

When we read what happened in the days of Noah—the penetration and the pressure of the occult, violence on Earth, and sexual deviance—it is interesting to note that corruption is the common denominator in all the signs and causes of what happened in that society. If we compare ourselves to those days, we find that things have changed very little, for you see and hear about it every day. To confirm this, let us answer the following questions. Has the occult and witchcraft penetrated our society? Yes, it has! Has there been a sustained and uninterrupted increase in sects during the last decades? Yes! Has the mind of all men become corrupt? Of course it has! Is violence, sexual degeneration, homosexuality, and lesbianism commonplace? Sadly, it is! Our society is very much like the one in Noah's time. This is the reason for the difficulties and crisis of our times and the main reason why God's judgment must come upon humanity.

Why is the world's economy in chaos? Why do we see judgment through earthquakes, tidal waves, floods, and hurricanes in our countries and cities? The answer is simple. If man becomes corrupt, the Earth becomes filled with violence, and by His righteousness, God must judge evil and corrupt men who refuse to repent from their sin.

Jesus spoke of the days of Lot.

"*28Likewise as it was also in the days of Lot: They ate, they drank, they bought, they sold, they planted, they built.*" Lucas 17:28

Jesus speaks of the days of Lot to compare their similarity to the end times.

"*4...men of Sodom, both old and young, all the people from every quarter, surrounded the house. 5And they called to Lot and said to him, 'Where are the men who came to you tonight? Bring them out to us that we may know them carnally.'*" Genesis 19:4, 5

Two angels went to Sodom to rescue Lot and his family, but when the people discovered their presence, they surrounded Lot's house. They wanted to *know* (*yada*), or have sex with, the two angels. The people's intense demands and aggression against Lot, that he may turn the two angels over to them, speaks much of just how corrupt Sodom was. It was a city dedicated to such an extreme form of sexual perversion that, to this day, the word sodomy is used to refer to homosexuality.

What is the sign we see in the days of Lot?

The sign of those times was an aggressive and violent form of homosexuality in men; this means they would openly and aggressively practice their homosexuality; they were by no means passive or ashamed of it. They sought out their victims with determination and violence and subjugated them forcefully. Another sign is that the entire population of Sodom, its elderly, adult, and the youth, were given to an aggressive and violent form of homosexuality; thus, ignoring the standards of conduct of that time. Do you see the similarity with today's society? The gay community of our time actively and aggressively imposes their conduct on our children in schools.

With this in mind, I invite you to consider current events in the United States, Latin America, and Europe. During the last decades, this tendency has increased rapidly, to such an extent that the governments of the world are actively looking for solutions without success.

What positive aspect can be redeemed from Noah and Lot's time?

The Word of God teaches that where sin abounds, grace also abounds, and that wherever iniquity abounds, the righteousness of God abounds as well. He always rescues the righteous who walk according to His laws.

God supernaturally warned His servants that judgment would come over the Earth.

As God's faithful servant, Noah received the supernatural revelation of what was to come and how he was to prepare to face it and survive.

"*7By faith Noah, being divinely warned of things not yet seen, moved with godly fear, prepared an ark for the saving of his household, by which he condemned the world and became heir of the righteousness which is according to faith." Hebrews 11:7*

Presently, we must also warn people of the bad events, catastrophes, judgments, or earthquakes that are to come. That is why God has placed His apostles and prophets in the midst of His people; to declare what is to come, what has been revealed by the Holy Spirit, and to provide a means of escape to those that fear the Lord. In the midst of all of this, God warns His faithful servants and shows us the way to survive and prosper through even the most devastating catastrophe.

"³And these things they will do to you because they have not known the Father nor Me." John 16:3

One of the ministries of the Holy Spirit is to tell us only what we need to survive and to fulfill God's purpose. This is the word for today: "In the midst of all that is happening today, adversity, corruption of the human character, sexual and moral corruption, and divine judgment, the Father will always show His people a way to survive. He will send the ravens with His provision and will give us peace and protection in the eye of the storm."

God sent angels to protect and deliver Lot

God sent His angels to protect and deliver Abraham's nephew and his family, and the Lord will do the same for us. He will send His angels or His supernatural presence, if necessary.

"14Are they not all ministering spirits sent forth to minister for those who will inherit salvation?" Hebrews 1:14

What signs did Jesus give regarding the end times?

"5For many will come in My name, saying, 'I am the Christ,' and will deceive many. 6And you will hear of wars and rumors of wars. See that you are not troubled; for all these things must come to pass, but the end is not yet. 7For nation will rise against nation, and kingdom against kingdom. And there will be famines, pestilences, and earthquakes in various places." Matthew 24:5-7

International wars, earthquakes, famines, and pestilences are the signs that Jesus said would occur in the end times. Please note the following: No one, no human being or angels in heaven, knows when the end will come except for God the Father. Only He knows the day (Mark 13:32). Although we may not have this date, we can look around and see if these signs are manifesting today. Let's review them one by one.

* **International Wars**

  The twentieth and twenty-first centuries have been particularly belligerent in the history of humanity. The human, social, and economic consequences of both World Wars, as well as the conflicts in the Near and Middle East are unprecedented[2]. The technology factor has been very important in the amount of harm generated. Meanwhile, the increase in aggressiveness

---

[2] Ralph Dahrendorf El recomienzo de la historia: de la caída del muro a la guerra de Irak, (Buenos Aires, Katz, 2006)

can be understood upon observing that, thus far in this century alone, almost ten conflicts have arisen with geostrategic impact and international reach.

- 1904-1905 Territorial war between Russia and Japan
- 1911-1912 Territorial war between Italy and Turkey
- 1912-1913 Balkan War: Greece, Bulgaria, Serbia, and Montenegro versus Turkey
- 1914-1918 World War I - France, England, Russia, Japan, Italy, Romania, and the United States versus Germany, Austria-Hungary, Turkey, and Bulgaria
- 1931 War for the Manchurian territory between Japan and China
- 1932-1935 Chaco War between Paraguay and Bolivia
- 1935 War for the Abyssinian territory between Italy and Ethiopia
- 1939-1940 Soviet / Finnish War
- 1939-1945 World War II: Axis (Japan, Germany, and Italy) vs. Allies (France, England, Russia, United States, and others)
- 1947-1949 First Arab-Israeli War between Israelis and Palestinian Arabs
- 1947-1949 First Indo-Pakistani War
- 1950-1953 Korean War: communist vs. pro-westerners
- 1954-1962 Algerian War: Independents vs. France
- 1955-75 Vietnam War: communist North vs. Pro-western South

- 1956 Suez/Sinai War : Jordan, Egypt, and Syria vs. Israel
- 1961-2000 Eritrean Independence War: East Africa vs. Ethiopia
- 1962 Cuban Missile Crisis: USA and USSR at the verge of World War III
- 1965-1966 Second Indo-Pakistani War
- 1967 Six Day War: June 4th thru 10th: Israel vs. Egypt, Jordan, Syria, and Iraq
- 1971 Third Indo-Pakistani War
- 1973 Yom Kippur War: Egypt and Syria vs. Israel
- 1978-1992 Afghanistan War: Communist government and USSR vs. Islamic guerrillas
- 1980-1988 Iran-Iraq War
- 1982 Falkland Islands War: Argentina vs. England
- 1983 US invasion of Grenada (Caribbean)
- Dec 1989-Feb 1990 US invasion of Panama
- 1991 Persian Gulf War: United Nations vs. Iraq
- 1991-1995: Yugoslav War of Independence: Serbs vs. Bosnians, Croats, Albanians with the intervention of the UN
- 1995 Ecuadorian-Peruvian War: Peru vs Ecuador
- 1996 Iraq War: USA vs. Iraq
- 1998-2003 Second Congo War
- 1999-Second Chechen War
- 2001-Present: War in Afghanistan
- 2001-Present: War against the axis of evil
- 2003-Present: War in Iraq
- 2005-Present: Chadian-Sudanese conflict
- 2006 Israel-Lebanon War

- 2006 Somali Civil War (international presence)[3]
- 2008 Russia-Georgia War
- 2008-2009 Gaza Strip Conflict
- 2009- Present: War tension between the USA and other western nations against North Korea and Iran due to their steps toward nuclear armament.

* **Natural Disasters**

Earthquakes, tidal waves, volcanic eruptions, hurricanes, floods, cyclones, and other epidemic disasters were announced by Jesus as signs of the last days. The *International Strategy for Disaster Reduction* is an organization that has documented that from 1900 to 2005 there were 9,821hydro-meteorological, geological, and biological disasters, not including the ones that were due to technical problems or human error. The most relevant piece of information is that more than half of them (5,210) occurred just in the last ten (10) years, of which 40 percent happened on the Asian continent. I have selected the better-known natural disasters of the last two centuries:

- 1902 Eruption of Mt. Pelado, Martinique
- 1906 Earthquake and wildfires in San Francisco, CA
- 1960 Earthquake and tsunami in Chile

---

[3] Javier Paredes (coordinator), *Historia Universal contemporánea 2. De la primera guerra mundial a nuestros días* (Barcelona, Ariel 2008); Juan Francisco Fuentes, *Historia universal del siglo XX: de la primera guerra mundial al ataque de las torres gemelas* (Madrid, Síntesis 2001); Dan Smith et al *Atlas del estado de la guerra y la paz* (Madrid, Akal, 1999.

- 1970 Earthquake in Peru
- 1985 Earthquake in Mexico City
- 1990 Earthquake in Iran
- 1991 Eruption of the Hudson volcano in Chile
- 1992 Earthquake in Flower Island, Indonesia
- 1998 Earthquakes in Afghanistan
- 1999 Earthquakes in Turkey
- 2001 Earthquake in Gujarat, India
- 2003 Earthquake in southeastern Iran
- 2004 Indian Ocean Tsunami
- 2004 Earthquake in Sumatra, Indonesia
- 2004 Hurricanes Charley, Francesca, Ivan , and Jean
- 2005 Hurricane Katrina
- 2005 Hurricane Stan
- 2005 Hurricane Wilma
- 2005 Earthquake in Cachemira, India
- 2007 Hurricane Dean
- 2007 Earthquake in Peru
- 2008 Flooding in Tabasco, Mexico
- 2008 Cyclone Nargis in Burma
- 2008 Earthquake in Sichuan
- 2009 Multiple earthquakes in Abruzzo, Italy[4]

In conclusion, although regular recurrence of earthquakes has generally been on the rise, said recurrence is less frequent since 1980.[5] Though there were none

[4] Information taken from the *Archive of Hurricane Seasons* (National Hurricane Center) www.nhc.noaa.gov; *World Report of disasters by the Red Cross* www.cruzroja.org, of the *International Strategy for Disaster Reduction* www.unisdr.org y *El País*, 16 of August 2007.

[5] Information taken from the *International Strategy for Disaster Reduction* www.unisdr.org/disaster-statistics/occurrence-trends-century.htm

for entire decades, there have been at least four in the last decades with devastating results. Moreover, the frequency of flooding has increased from about 50 per year in the first part of the 1980's to currently more than 200 per year.[6]

* **Famines**

In its study, *The state of Food Insecurity in the World 2008*, the Food and Agriculture Organization of the United Nations (FAO-UN), estimates that 25,000 people including children and adults, die every day.[7] It calculates that almost one billion people suffer chronic hunger or malnutrition, and that these long-term tendencies, in and of themselves alarming, have worsened the last two years as a consequence of the economic crisis and the rise in prices.

Close to two thirds of the population in said condition are located in India, China, the Democratic Republic of Congo, Bangladesh, Indonesia, Pakistan, and Ethiopia. However, there is no region in the world that does not face the problem of deaths due to malnutrition and the like, chief among them are Africa, Asia, and the Latin-American subcontinent. Additionally, a third of infant mortality worldwide is

---

[6] Centro para la Investigación de la Epidemiología de los Desastres (2008), *Disaster data: a balanced perspective*, Bélgica, UCL, CRED Crunch, 11: 1-2.

[7] FAO Corporate (2008), *The state of food insecurity in the world 2008*, FAO-United Nations.

due to malnutrition[8]. Most surprisingly, according to the FAO's study, world hunger grew despite a global increase in wealth and food production as never before seen in the past decade. The effects of this unfortunate phenomenon are expressed in levels of inequality, oppression, generation of social revolts, as well as in an ever increasing dehumanization, inability of governments to revert the tendency, and the appearance of other types of ills such as pestilences and epidemics.

• **Pestilence**

One of the best-known historic facts that we have knowledge of is the black or bubonic plague which struck Europe in the fourteenth century and took the lives of a third of its population. It is dramatic to see that for the past quarter century a flurry of lethal epidemics and pandemics have begun to gradually flourish. AIDS, malaria, tuberculosis, and infectious diseases have claimed the lives of millions of people all around the planet. A third of deaths in the world are due to said causes[9] and highly-contagious new viruses are affecting the world population as well.

The recent swine flu or influenza virus A (H1N1), with reported cases in 74 countries, supports this affirmation and is profiled as evidence of what Jesus

---

[8] World Health Organization (2009), *Global Sanitary Statistics 2009*, WHO.
[9] World Health Organization (2009), *Global Sanitary Statistics 2009. Mortality and Morbility by SpecificCauses*, WHO, pp.47-ss.

predicted. Even as this epidemic spread rapidly towards the end of April 2009, particularly in Mexico and the United States, the World Health Organization decided in June of the same year to elevate the pandemic alert scale to level 6, the highest level. This indicated that the influenza was not merely propagating, but rather that it was the first in 40 years that had spread to such a magnitude that it was no longer possible to restrict it to a particular geographic area[10].

Though science, strategic planning, and technology have evolved at a dizzying pace, I am convinced that, when the moment comes, they will prove to be insufficient to face the challenges of increasingly aggressive, intense, and massive epidemics to come.

♦ **Christians will be persecuted and hated by this world.**

"⁹Then they will deliver you up to tribulation and kill you, and you will be hated by all nations for My name's sake."
Matthew 24:9

Jesus warned us about this. Opposition to Him did not end with His crucifixion. Persecution of His ideas and of His followers would extend throughout the centuries, particularly where Christianity would attempt to gain ground. The book of Acts narrates the challenges that the primitive church had to face and suffer. Stephen, Jacob, Peter, Paul, Barnabas, Silas, and Luke

---

[10] World Health Organization, *Weekly epidemiological record*, 84:25, June 19, 2004, 249-60.

head the list of those persecuted for propagating the Gospel of Jesus. Thousands more, whose names are not registered by history, met the same fate either simultaneously or subsequently.

Multiple reliable sources document that since the first centuries, especially under the emperors Decius and Valerian, the siege and extermination of Christians was brutal.[11] For 1500 years, Asia and Africa were forbidden territory for the expression of Christianity. In the past two centuries, Sudan, communist Europe, China, North Korea, Ethiopia, Nigeria, Uganda, and countries under Islamic extremism have massacred Christians with the consent of its governments. Though some countries have become more flexible today in their position regarding Christianity, or rather have legalized freedom of religion as a result of their move towards democracy, in many nations, preaching the Gospel continues to be a dangerous occupation. A recent book compiles testimonies regarding the persecution of Christians suffer today in Turkey, Iraq, Jordan, Syria, and Lebanon[12]. This serves as but one show of the evidence that thousands of women and men are suffering right now for the cause of the name of Jesus.

---

[11] Reinhard Selinger (2002), *The mid-third century persecutions of Decius and Valerian*, Frankfurt-am-Main, Peter Lang. A general visión in Joaquín Gómez-Pantoja (2003), *Ancient History: Greece and Rome*, Barcelona, Joaquín Mortíz.

[12] Rodolfo Casadei (2008), *Il sangue dell'agnello. Reportage fra i cristiani perseguitati in Medio Oriente* (The blood of the Lamb. Report by Christians suffering persecution in the Middle East), Milan, Guerinni e Associati.

• **Apostasy, betrayal among Christians, and false prophets.**

"[10]And then many will be offended, will betray one another, and will hate one another. [11]Then many false prophets will rise up and deceive many." Matthew 24:10, 11

When difficult moments come and Christians are persecuted, many of them will leave the faith and even betray their brethren. The Barna Group (a company that specializes in conducting research for churches), conducted a survey in the United States and found that Christians have changed their perspective regarding the truthfulness of Christianity. Half of the adults in the study consider said system of beliefs to be only one of many options that Americans can choose from. Meanwhile, an enormous majority of adults select what they will believe in, instead of embracing a church or a denominational system of beliefs[13].

Regarding *false messiahs*, it is important to note that some Jewish references calculate that, since the resurrection of Jesus to the present day, there have been more than 44 people claiming to be the Christ or Messiah.

The invasion of *liberal Christianity*, which modifies the message of Jesus[14], and the acceptance of supposed

---

[13] Barna Group (2009), *Americans are exploring new ways of experiencing God*, en www.barna.org/faith/spirituality.

[14] Stephen Mansfield. *The faith of Barack Obama* (Nashville, Thomas Nelson. 2008)

prophets that base themselves on "sacred texts" different from biblical principles are in the same category. Added to this is the unfounded criticism we hear every day, in all communication mediums, against Christian leaders that teach according to the Gospel of Christ. These act as a living testimony of the state of the world, and can all be interpreted as the signs that Jesus said would take place in the end times.

+ **The love of many believers will grow cold due to the absence of law.**

"12 And because lawlessness will abound, the love of many will grow cold." Matthew 24:12

The intense pressure of evil or iniquity will cause the love of many believers to grow cold towards God or others.

❧❧❧

*The absence of law conduces
to the loss of love.*

❧❧❧

The love of God is not that you do what you want, when you want, and the way you want to do it; that is the world's notion of love. God's love requires discipline and self control because it is not selfish.

Two strong supernatural pressures over modern society:

+ **The satanic spiritual pressure of the occult**

"¹Now the Spirit expressly says that in latter times some will depart from the faith, giving heed to deceiving spirits and doctrines of demons." 1 Timothy 4:1

Deceptive demons cause many believers to leave their churches.

• **The progressive degeneration of the human character**

There is a list of 18 moral failings that further degrade our society each day. Their root is selfishness. Men are lovers of themselves, of pleasure, and of money. This is the condition of the world and of mankind in the end times.

While this happens, what is God doing in the Church?

God is pouring of His spirit.

"¹⁵For these are not drunk, as you suppose, since it is only the third hour of the day. ¹⁶But this is what was spoken by the prophet Joel: ¹⁷'And it shall come to pass in the last days, says God, that I will pour out of My Spirit on all flesh; your sons and your daughters shall prophesy, your young men shall see visions, your old men shall dream dreams. ¹⁸And on My menservants and on My maidservants I will pour out My Spirit in those days; and they shall prophesy.'" Acts 2:15-18

The outpour of rain in the natural represents the outpour of the Holy Spirit in the supernatural.

"23Be glad then, you children of Zion, and rejoice in the LORD your God; for He has given you the former rain faithfully, and He will cause the rain to come down for you—The former rain, and the latter rain in the first month." Joel 2:23

The rain will come down in two seasons:

* **The former rain**

    This begins in Israel at the end of summer and the start of winter, and only falls in some places.

* **The latter rain**

    It comes at the end of the winter season and falls over the entire nation.

What is the rain like in Israel?

There are only two rainy seasons in Israel—one in the summer and the other in winter. The climate is completely dry during the summer, lasting more or less from April to November. It does not rain at all during these months. At the end of the dry season, which is the beginning of winter, what is called the "former rain" begins to fall. That rain falls a bit over a region or over another, a little here and a little there. It does not fall abundantly over the entire country, but only in certain places, until winter comes. By that time, what is called the essential "latter rain" is anticipated. It is the greatest rainfall of the year and encompasses the nation of Israel.

We have learned of what God is doing with the Church and of what He has done throughout history. While corruption grows and difficult times come, God pours out of His spirit upon all flesh. This is hope for those of us who are His children.

The former rain fell over the primitive Church in Jerusalem—after Christ's ascension; that lasted about a century. It affected the universal Church throughout the world and it was a supernatural visitation of the Holy Spirit. Thereafter began the summer of the history of the Church. The Holy Spirit has not been totally poured out yet. There has been an outpouring in some parts of the world, some drops here and other drops there, first in Europe, then in America, and later in Africa. The Holy Spirit has always been active. He has poured Himself upon a group, a race, a culture, but there has not been a great outpouring of rain that has affected all of the Church in the entire world.

Today we are moving towards winter, the time of the greatest outpouring of the Holy Spirit over the entire world, which will fall over all the Church. It is the restoration of God's supernatural power in the Church and the fulfillment of the final prophecy. We need to understand that we are living in the times of the latter rain and should expect it. Not everything is bad news. The signs are not all bad. One of the signs of the last days is what God is doing—the outpour of His Holy Spirit upon all flesh.

Dear reader, if you live in sin, if your mind is corrupted, if your thoughts are perverse, or if you practice the homosexual lifestyle, the occult, or violence, then today is the day for change. God offers to open your eyes through the Holy Spirit so that you may know Jesus Christ, receive the gift of the Holy Spirit, and be filled with Him in order to begin a new life in the midst of adversity.

God is pouring of Himself over every nation with a heavy rain and a global revival. It is God's supernatural power being poured out in miracles, healings, and wonders. He is doing this because where there is much sin, the mercy of God also abounds. Where there is injustice, the Lord lifts up His righteousness.

The Bible says that he who is holy should further sanctify himself, and that whoever is pure should purify himself even more. What I am saying is that this is an opportunity for God to fill you with His Holy Spirit. Take advantage of it!

Summary:

• The Earth is full of violence, corruption, and sexual perversion due to the pressure and intense penetration of the occult and of the universal corruption of the human mind.

• The Earth is under a curse because of the violence and murders that have resulted in bloodshed, and is due to the victims' resulting in a quest for revenge.

• Only the blood of Christ can end this curse. We need Jesus!

- The times today are like those in the days of Lot. Sexual perversion has multiplied.

- God warns His servants of forthcoming judgment and grants the opportunity for repentance.

- God sends His angels to protect His children.

- We are living the fulfillment of the signs that Jesus said we would see when the end times drew near. There are wars and rumors of them, natural disasters, famine, the multiplication of evil, persecution of the Church, false prophets, the occult, and the love of believers that has grown cold.

- The two greatest supernatural pressures of modern society are the satanic pressure that comes from the occult and the progressive degeneration of the human character.

- While all this happens, God is pouring of His Spirit.

- God's rain will come in two seasons, the former rain and the latter rain.

If you are reading this book and are a believer, rejoice! Raise your head! Even though these bad things are taking place at this time, God is pouring of His Spirit. If you have never been filled by the Holy Spirit, I pray that as you read this book He pours of Himself on you, that God's rain falls over your life, and that, as proof, you begin to speak in other tongues right now.

"Father, I pray for those believers who have never received the rain and power of the Holy Spirit with the evidence of speaking in other tongues. Let them be filled right now and may they receive that latter rain in abundance over their lives! Let them receive the rain that gives them hope for a glorious future in the name of Jesus. Amen and amen."

CHAPTER III

❧❧❧

The Corruption of Human Character

❧❧❧

The root of all the problems in the world is mankind's Self—self-sufficiency, independence, or the ego; this is nothing more than humanity's effort to live completely independent of God while still trying to get close to Him on its own terms and strength. There are certain questions that psychologists, psychiatrists, researchers, and even philosophers ask regarding the root of the Self in the eternal quest to know how to deal with it effectively. Most religions do it through rules, by observing certain holy days, festivals, ceremonies, and all that is entailed therein to deny their ego in order to become a good person. This is nothing more that human effort.

Among the efforts of religions, philosophy, and psychology, we find three affirmations regarding the ego. They are *know yourself*, *accept yourself*, and *express yourself*. I completely disagree with these affirmations of modern psychology and of religion. Why? What is wrong with them? I will further explain in light of revealed biblical knowledge.

+ **Know yourself**

   How can a human being know or study himself, in regards to him and others, in a strictly material environment when everything related to the Earth is void of eternal meaning?

Animals may feel satisfied with this world but man will never be while he is at odds with God, his Creator and Redeemer. My argument is that man can only get to know himself when he compares himself to God, and this can only happen strictly by divine revelation. His revelation is required for mankind to understand origin and nature. It will not come through modern psychology, reasoning, or psychiatry. You will not be able to know yourself unless you do so from the standpoint of your image and likeness to God.

Allow me to say it this way. You are a child of God in the process of being made into the likeness of Jesus, the most perfect and influential person that has ever existed in this or any other planet. Only when that happens can you know yourself. Any other psychological, philosophical, or religious knowledge, good as it may be, is only partial or marginal because it only affects the limits of the ego or of the Self. The most that secular psychology can do is to improve the ego, or self love, which actually destroys us because it separates us from Jesus and His complete salvation. It is therefore impossible to know ourselves without God's revelation. Getting to know who we are begins with comparing ourselves to the image and likeness of God—the Self does not know itself because it does not know God.

* **Accept yourself**

How can the Self accept what it is if it is full of conflicts, contradictions, inferiorities, guilt, or unresolved issues? To ask a human being to accept himself in such a state is impossible. Should he somehow be able to accept himself in such a condition, he will always live in a state of disatisfaction.

Illustration: A man wrote to a tennis club to terminate his membership stating, "I cannot continue to be a part of a club that accepts people like me."

Man has standards, so to ask him to accept himself produces rebellion in him. He will only be able to accept himself when he has changed or is in the process of change. When secular psychology asks a person to accept him or herself in their present state, it is denying God and the person's conscience.

We can accept ourselves only when we recognize the new man that Jesus Christ raises up within us. God's Word is clear when it says that the old man was crucified with Christ and buried with Him in baptism. Therefore, I cannot accept that old man in my life because I can only accept the new man, made through the work of Jesus Christ at the Cross of Calvary and through a new birth.

* **Express yourself**

The advice of modern psychology points to the presumption of the ego that we should put ourselves as the center of all. However, anything that places man at the center is in reality off-center because it feeds the egocentrism and the self-sufficiency that are precisely the ailments that it tries to cure.

What happens with psychology's three affirmations? What is missing? They are missing what the Christian faith offers, i.e., the execution and death of the ego on the Cross. Time and time again, the Bible commands us to crucify the ego and not to exalt it nor to make of it the center of our existence. The Lord said that mankind was created a bit less important than the angels. Man was created in God's image and likeness but it was never His intention for man to become God. That is religion's central sin, the attempt of the Self to usurp God's throne.

∾∾∾

The usurpation of God's throne by the Self
is the central sin of religion and the maximum
expression of presumption and of sin.

∾∾∾

The prideful claim of pretending to be God is the sin that made Lucifer fall from the highest to the lowest. Just like my fingers are deeply rooted to the palm of my hand, so are external sins to desires not surrendered or executed at the Cross.

Illustration: Why do we get angry or have a fit of rage? It is because someone messed with our Self. Why are we dishonest and lie? It is because we think this will benefit the Self. Why are we impure? It is because we think of giving pleasure to the Self. Why do we feel envy or jealousy? It is because someone went ahead of our Self. All of the mentioned sins are only the fruit. The unyielding Self is the root. External sins are only symptoms of the cause. The rebellious Self that never submits provokes these symptoms; that is why there are doctors trying to deal with the symptoms before dealing with the cause and thus do not achieve a positive effect over the illness. If we do not want sin to take hold of us, we need to fight the ego God's way.

The Christian faith is radical because it goes to the root of all problems, both individual and collective, through dealing with the ego and taking it to the Cross, crucifying it, and allowing it to die.

Illustration: One time Peter told Jesus, "We left everything to follow you. What is our reward?" Surely they had left it all; all except the Self. His thinking of a reward and asking for it exposed him. His Self was still alive.

What happens to the Self when it is not thoroughly put to death?

"38And he who does not take his cross and follow after Me is not worthy of Me. 39He who finds his life will lose it, and he who loses his life for My sake will find it." Matthew 10:38, 39

Jesus said this, "Whosoever finds his life will lose it." If we concentrate on our Self, our lives will disintegrate.

そうそう

*Every person that concentrates on his or herself
is equivalent to a person that is disintegrating.*

そうそう

If you concentrate on yourself, you will end up not liking yourself and no one else will like you either. The rest of the verse is just as true, "He who loses his life for My sake, will find it." Lose yourself in the will of God, in His like-ness, in being like Jesus. Surrender yourself and then you will find yourself. This is a paradox but if you surrender to God you will find complete freedom.

❧❧❧

You will never own yourself more completely than when you completely belong to God.

❧❧❧

The only role of a human being is to maintain his will in line to God's will in total submission and obedience. He should deny his Self daily; thus, denying what he thinks, feels, and wants in order to reach whatsoever God thinks, feels, and wants. When he does this, God's grace comes to his assistance to enable him to lead and maintain a pure and holy life.

Is there something wrong in Jesus asking us to deny ourselves? Is it death and not life? Yes, there is death but it is death to the false manner of living and to the false Self that we had exalted before we came to Jesus. When Paul said, "....I am crucified with Christ..." what he meant was the world and its falsehood were crucified. He did not say that his true Self, the new man, should be eliminated. This we know because the verse continues, "I no longer live...." Paul was cleansed by the crucifixion of the false Self, the body of death, the flesh, the ego which previously sustained him. A new man was resurrected as a man of God and, therefore, he was alive. That is why he said,

"...for Christ that lives within me.", because he felt truly alive in every cell of his body and of his mind. He was alive! He went from death to life.

❧❧❧

We do not know what it is to be alive
until we attend our own funeral.

❧❧❧

The text that speaks of the death and resurrection of Paul can be read the following way, "I have been crucified with Christ. I have died to all selfish purposes in my life. With Christ I am jointly crucified. I no longer live. I have been born in to Christ's purpose in me. Christ lives within me. Christ in me, the hope of glory!"

With Jesus we have fullness of life and we merge our interests and all our being in the life of another. "The life which I now live in the flesh I live by the faith of the Son of God." This material existence is not life; it is certainly artificial, operating in the flesh within and through the material. However, the pattern of my life is that of the Son of God and the power of my life is in His name.

❧❧❧

The crucifixion of Jesus
is resurrection within us.

❧❧❧

What is the cause or root of man's corrupt character?

"*¹But know this, that in the last days perilous times will come: ²For men will be lovers of themselves, lovers of money, boasters,*

proud, blasphemers, disobedient to parents, unthankful, unholy,
³unloving, unforgiving, slanderers, without self-control, brutal,
despisers of good, ⁴traitors, headstrong, haughty, lovers of pleasure
rather than lovers of God, ⁵having a form of godliness but denying
its power. And from such people turn away! ⁶For of this sort are
those who creep into households and make captives of gullible
women loaded down with sins, led away by various lusts, ⁷always
learning and never able to come to the knowledge of the truth."
2 Timothy 3:1-7

In some versions, the expression *dangerous times* is translated as *terrible times*. If there were ever a period in which
that was a reality, it is today. We are living in dangerous
and terrible times and that is why Paul told Timothy,
"...but know this..."

Why does Paul emphasize that?

The apostle knew human nature was facing imminent degradation that would result in bringing God's judgment
over humanity. Although some people do not believe in
that judgment, it will come nonetheless. Said judgment
will come in three stages: a preliminary judgment, an immediate judgment, and a final judgment. I believe we have
entered the time of the preliminary judgment.

Why will those latter days come?

The reason for this season of judgment is the corruption
or degradation the human race has suffered and continues
to suffer. With regards to this, there are some important

points that must be explained in order to better understand this topic.

◆ The corruption or degradation of the human character

The apostle Paul correctly analyzes the main cause of God's judgment on Earth as being the corruption or degradation of the human character; when this takes place, there will be no need to blame the government, religion, or other people or institutions because the main cause is the degradation of the human character.

Paul lists the 18 character flaws that would characterize the people of the end times. In that list, there is nothing that is foreign to our generation. The human race is in that condition today. Men today are lovers of themselves and lovers of money. They are boasters, disobedient to parents, proud, blasphemers, unthankful, unholy, unloving, unforgiving, slanderers, without self control, brutal, despisers of good, traitors, headstrong, haughty, and lovers of pleasure rather than lovers of God.

◆ Corruption is irreversible

Illustration: An apple will corrupt and rot with time. Its corruption may take time, but it will happen.

৵৵৵
*Moral, ethical, and physical
corruptions are irreversible.*
৵৵৵

Once corruption becomes part of a person, organization, or group of people, it cannot be reversed. Only God could change said situation by His power. However, His plan is not to apply a patch, to fix up, or improve corruption nor is it to cover up sin like religion does. His plan instead includes a radical, lasting, and permanent transformation. It implies the formation of a new person, a new creation, and a complete restoration of what was corrupt. This He does by changing the heart of man.

"[17]Therefore, if anyone is in Christ, he is a new creation; old things have passed away; behold, all things have become new." 2 Corinthians 5:17

☙☙☙☙

God will not only produce a change
but will make all things new.

☙☙☙☙

"[13]...according to His promise, look for new heavens and a new earth in which righteousness dwells." 2 Peter 3:13

Corruption is irreversible in this country and in this society. Although it may be hard to accept this fact, mankind becomes more corrupt with each passing day.

• **The root of corruption and of moral degradation is the "love of the ego".**

Selfishness or egocentrism means to place ourselves first; to consider our needs and wants above those of others. Let us analyze the following verse.

"⁵Having a form of godliness but denying its power. And from such people turn away!" 2 Timothy 3:5

What is the power or efficiency of godliness?

Godliness is the supernatural power of God's grace to change a person's character. It is the supernatural power of the Spirit that deals with selfishness or the love of the Self. This power can change a selfish, egocentric person into a loving, kind, and gentle one.

Though we have gifts, talents, abilities, and we speak in tongues, if we do not believe in godliness and in the supernatural grace of God to change our character, we are denying its power. Religion preaches godliness but it is only an outward appearance as it lacks the power to change the root of man's selfishness. Religion adds patches, forces discipline, and invents and implements rules and laws to halt corruption; however, it cannot change man's heart. Only the power of God's supernatural grace is capable of doing so.

Every human being hungers for power. The soul naturally hungers for it. Sociologists say that the desire for power is mankind's greatest motivation. It is not wrong to desire power as God made mankind to govern and have dominion over the Earth with the supernatural power of the Kingdom. What is wrong is to desire that power to satisfy the egocentrism that dominates us. We must desire the correct power; one that works and changes lives, particularly the power that changes selfish people into loving and good.

We should desire the power of mercy and the supernatural power of God's *grace*.

Is there selfishness in the Church or in the family? Is there selfishness in our families? If we don't deal with selfishness it will be the beginning of our corruption and if we fail to eliminate it, it will continue to grow until it completely corrupts us. We must, therefore, ask God to deliver us from selfishness.

What is the result of "loving the ego" or self love?

The country I now live in is not the same as it was twenty years ago. The Barna Group,[15] which is geared towards the investigation of spiritual matters, published statistics that show alarming facts of what happens in the span of a day in the United States.

- 2,753 adolescents become pregnant
- 1,899 women have an abortion
- 367 women suffer a miscarriage
- 1,287 adolescents give birth
- 72 babies die during their first month of life
- 110 babies die after their first year of life
- 9 babies die due to gun fire.
- 5 adolescents commit suicide
- 100 adolescents contract gonorrhea or syphilis
- 988 children are sexually abused
- 3,288 children run away from home
- 49,322 children are in juvenile correctional facilities
- 2,269 illegitimate children are born

---

[15] www.Barma.org

• 2,989 children's parents divorce

In the Bible, there is a phrase that appears from time to time ..."but God". God has the answer for all kinds of moral corruption.

How should we respond in dangerous times?

• **Recognize that these times confirm what the Scriptures say.** We should say, "Thank you, God!", as the Bible is the truth that already advised us of all that is happening now. Though these times are difficult, they confirm the veracity of the Scriptures so we can therefore trust and be happy. Likewise, we can also have a solid hope that the promises of salvation and redemption will come to pass as well. The Word of God never lies.

• **Deal with the root of the problem which is "love of the ego".** Only the power of mercy or God's supernatural grace can change a selfish individual into a loving, selfless, generous, and just person.

How should we deal with the ego?

"[24]...Jesus said to His disciples, 'If anyone desires to come after Me, let him deny himself, and take up his cross, and follow Me. [25]For whoever desires to save his life will lose it, but whoever loses his life for My sake will find It.'"
Matthew 16:24, 25

The simplest definition of being a Christian is a person who follows Jesus; to do it effectively we must:

- **Deny self.** Remember what we spoke about in the introduction, the egocentric Self must die so that Christ, the image and likeness of the Father, may live. The new man, the new purified Self, is who should live.

- **Take up the cross.** That is the place where the Self is executed. You can attempt to follow Jesus but you will not be able to until you meet both of the above conditions.

෨෨෨

We must die in order to live.

෨෨෨

What does it mean to deny self?

Denying self consists of dealing with the love of the ego. The ego might say, "I want. I think. I feel. Help me. Pray for me. Heal me." However, you can silence it. To deny self means to say "no" to what you want, feel, or think but to say "yes" to God and to the needs of others.

෨෨෨

The majority of people that have
ongoing problems are selfish.

෨෨෨

What is your cross?

Your cross is where your will meet with God's will. You cannot follow Jesus doing your own will. It is impossible. The Cross is where we die to the ego.

"¹¹And they overcame him by the blood of the Lamb and by the word of their testimony, and they did not love their lives to the death." Revelations 12:11

They are the people, like you and me, which have believed in Christ. Who did we overcome? Satan. How did we overcome him? We did so by the blood of the Lamb and the word of our testimony. We defeat Satan when we testify regarding what the Word says and what the blood of Christ did in our lives. When it says that "...they did not love their lives to the death", it means that being alive was not an essential priority for them. Their priority was to do the will of God whether they remained alive or not. The last phrase says, "They underestimated their lives to the death" while another translation says, "they did not love their lives to the death".

Satan does not fear our theology. He does, however, fear our commitment. Committed Christians are the ones that make him tremble because they are agents of change and salvation.

What does it mean to be committed?

To commit means to deny ourselves and to take up

the cross; only after doing so can we follow Jesus. This is radical.

❧❧❧

God's solution to the ego
is to execute it at the Cross.

❧❧❧

* Tribulation draws us closer to God.

* In times of tribulation, affliction, or adversity, there are some people that rebel and hardened their hearts, but yet others will seek God more than ever.

Many never thought about seeking God during the good times, but they do so during a crisis time. One reason why God allows tribulation to take place is for His people to turn towards Him.

"26Men's hearts failing them from fear and the expectation of those things which are coming on the earth, for the powers of the heavens will be shaken." Luke 21:26

The opportune moment to communicate this truth to people is when their hearts become weak and begin to corrupt.

"14And this gospel of the kingdom will be preached in all the world as a witness to all the nations, and then the end will come." Matthew 24:14

The best time to share the Gospel of the kingdom to the entire world is during times of crises.

What is the response of believers? In the midst of all this darkness, our light shines through our good works, not by what we say.

"16Let your light so shine before men, that they may see your good works and glorify your Father in heaven." Matthew 5:16

Why does God tolerate evil? God's supreme purpose is that His people be purified through His grace unto every good work.

"11For the grace of God that brings salvation has appeared to all men, 12teaching us that, denying ungodliness and worldly lusts, we should live soberly, righteously, and godly in the present age, 13looking for the blessed hope and glorious appearing of our great God and Savior Jesus Christ, 14who gave Himself for us, that He might redeem us from every lawless deed and purify for Himself His own special people, zealous for good works." Titus 2:11-14

What is the word of comfort for us?

"16For all that is in the world—the lust of the flesh, the lust of the eyes, and the pride of life—is not of the Father but is of the world. 17And the world is passing away, and the lust of it; but he who does the will of God abides forever." 1 John 2:16, 17

In the midst of a changing, evil, and unstable world, all things will pass away except one: the person that does the will of God and is joined to it will remain forever.

How can we be free of the ego?

The initial and fundamental step to be free of the ego is repentance. As we just read, the ego is the main cause, or the source, of moral corruption and the degradation of human character. We must recognize our condition before God and tell Him with all our heart, *"Lord, I am a selfish and egocentric person. My life begins and ends with me. Everything I do is centered on me but I am tired of being this way. This has not brought me anything good nor has it made me happy. Heavenly Father, I want to change. Make me free of this bondage! I want to be free! Help me to deny myself, to take up my cross, and to follow You."*

Most people can identify with this because this is one of the greatest problems the Church has, i.e., the love of ego, or being selfish or egocentric. God will loosen His supernatural grace and His power over those that pray sincerely and want to live *right* each day.

In summary:

* The last days will come due to the corruption of the human character, the irreversibility of corruption, and to the love of ego.

* The power of *mercy* is based on converting a person from selfish and egocentric to loving and kind.
* Selfishness gives way to corruption, and we must deal with it before complete ruin takes hold.

* Love of the ego has driven this nation, and the entire world, into living difficult times.

* We must recognize that everything that happens confirms what the Scriptures say.

* In order to deal with the ego we must deny ourselves and take up our cross daily.

* The Cross is the place where our ego dies and where we do only the will of God.

* Tribulation is the most favorable time to speak to people about the Gospel of Christ.

CHAPTER IV

࿊࿊࿊

He Will Cause
All Things to Shake

࿊࿊࿊

B efore we get into the topic, I'd like to ask the following. Do you believe God is love? Do you believe God sends judgment? I ask because most people believe God is very loving but they do not believe in His judgment. I want to tell you that He does send judgment. Preachers don't like to speak of God in terms of Him as a judge because they think it would scare people, and they don't want their people to leave.

What is the function of the Holy Spirit on Earth, according to Jesus?

"8And when He has come, He will convict the world of sin, and of righteousness, and of judgment." John 16:8

The Holy Spirit carries out three activities on Earth:

- He convicts the world of the sin of not believing in Jesus; this is done so unbelievers will understand their need to repent and seek to restore their relationship with the Father.

- He convicts the world of righteousness by revealing the Father's righteousness through Jesus.

- He convicts the world of judgment by making us aware that Satan has already been judged by the sacrifice of Jesus.

"8...when He has come, He will convict the world of sin, and of righteousness, and of judgment: 9of sin, because they do not believe in Me; 10of righteousness, because I go to My Father and you see Me no more; 11of judgment, because the ruler of this world is judged." John 16:8-11

The same One who provided for our salvation also acts as Judge: His name is Jesus. Interestingly enough, the apostles always presented Jesus as Savior and Judge.

"42And He commanded us to preach to the people, and to testify that it is He who was ordained by God to be Judge of the living and the dead." Acts 10:42

Peter puts judgment ahead of forgiveness. The same One who granted us forgiveness of sins is also the One that judges all things.

"30... 'Vengeance is Mine, I will repay,' says the Lord. And again, 'The LORD will judge His people.' 31It is a fearful thing to fall into the hands of the living God." Hebrews 10.30, 31

Jesus was designated by the Father to judge and to save. He is as much the Judge as He is the Savior.

What is happening in the world today? Everything is being shaken and removed.

"26whose voice then shook the earth; but now He has promised, saying, 'Yet once more I shake not only the earth, but also heaven.' 27Now this, 'Yet once more,' indicates the removal of those things that are being shaken, as of things that are made, that the things

which cannot be shaken may remain. [28]Therefore, since we are receiving a kingdom which cannot be shaken, let us have grace, by which we may serve God acceptably with reverence and godly fear." Hebrews 12:26-28

What things will be shaken?

"[47]Whoever comes to Me, and hears My sayings and does them, I will show you whom he is like: [48]He is like a man building a house, who dug deep and laid the foundation on the rock. And when the flood arose, the stream beat vehemently against that house, and could not shake it, for it was founded on the rock. [49]But he who heard and did nothing is like a man who built a house on the earth without a foundation, against which the stream beat vehemently; and immediately it fell. And the ruin of that house was great." Luke 6:47-49

The apostles and prophets have spoken of what the Lord will shake, remove, and stir up during the coming years. Note there is no difference in the trials that each house mentioned in the above text underwent. Both were stricken by the storm. The fact that you are doing the will of God does not exempt you from incoming storms. Both houses experienced the same storm, but only the one built upon the rock survived it; the one that was built on the earth fell.

ॐॐॐ

Everything not built on hearing and doing
God's Word will be shaken.

ॐॐॐ

How do we build on the rock?

To build on the rock is to hear *and* obey God's Word. This is the only foundation that will hold a building firmly in place.

What can be shaken?

* **Your personal life**

    I have known of individuals whose lives were shaken due to illness, poverty, divorce, separation, bankruptcy, or the death of a loved one. Due to their individual crisis, they gave up because their lives were not built on the Rock—Jesus! They did not live according to the teaching of His Word. This, however, does not mean that if we build our lives on Jesus, we will never have problems. We will have them. The difference being that we will not be shaken, knocked down, or destroyed but rather we will have the strength to face and defeat whatever presents itself.

* **Divided families**

    "25But Jesus knew their thoughts, and said to them: 'Every kingdom divided against itself is brought to desolation, and every city or house divided against itself will not stand.'" Matthew 12:25

    The family that lacks unity, love, and peace can and will be shaken; we see it everyday, in the world and in the Church. The result of the destruction of the family is that children are abandoned. As a result, they grow up without love, identity or a sense of fatherhood. Any institution built on a foundation other than the teachings of Jesus will be shaken, and the home is no exeption.

* **The banking system**

This problem was diagnosed a long time ago. The external debt of the United States reaches $12.25 billion which is equivalent to $ 41,000 per person in a total population of three hundred million inhabitants. The way the economy is going, it is extremely difficult for this nation to escape bankruptcy. That is a fact.

* **Business and big corporations**

Companies in business for over a hundred years, as in the case of the automobile industry, are at the brink of bankruptcy or will be forced to merge with other companies to avoid a complete tragedy.

* **Governments are being shaken**

Many governments are deep in permanent processes of instability due to economic, political, religious, or cultural reasons. We have to take note of such things because we are used to considering these institutions as stable and solvent. However, there is no bank or corporation that is as secure and stable as it would seem.

+ **Religious institutions**

These do not have, nor can they give, any guarantee of, stability or security unless they are faithfully built on the teachings of Jesus. Institutions, councils, and well known so-called Christian men will be shaken. Do not look or cling to the banks, government, or big corporations. Do not seek your stability or safety from religious institutions. They cannot provide it as they too will be shaken.

+ **Physical structures or buildings**

"12For the day of the LORD of hosts shall come upon everything proud and lofty, upon everything lifted up—and it shall be brought low—13Upon all the cedars of Lebanon that are high and lifted up, and upon all the oaks of Bashan; 14upon all the high mountains, and upon all the hills that are lifted up; 15Upon every high tower, and upon every fortified wall." Isaiah 2:12-15

God hates arrogance and pride above all things; that is what has caused the violent shaking of all things.

"25There will be on every high mountain and on every high hill rivers and streams of waters, in the day of the great slaughter, when the towers fall." Isaiah 30:25

All the modern buildings we see around us will be shaken; all will fall one day. It will happen just as God said.

- **The Earth shall be moved**

"[12]I looked when He opened the sixth seal, and behold, there was a great earthquake; and the sun became black as sackcloth of hair, and the moon became like blood. [13]And the stars of heaven fell to the earth, as a fig tree drops its late figs when it is shaken by a mighty wind. [14]Then the sky receded as a scroll when it is rolled up, and every mountain and island was moved out of its place." Revelations 6:12-14

- **The earth will be shaken**

Nothing or no one is exempt of being shaken. The heavens, Earth, and everything that can be shaken will be shaken. God wants to show there is only one thing or entity that cannot be shaken: His Kingdom. One way of doing this will be to allow everything that is fleeting and unstable to be shaken. Our security is not in any of the things we just studied, but rather, in the unshakable Kingdom of God.

How will this unshakable Kingdom be established?

"[1]Behold, the LORD makes the earth empty and makes it waste, distorts its surface and scatters abroad its inhabitants. [2]And it shall be: as with the people, so with the priest; as with the servant, so with his master; as with the maid, so with her mistress; as with the buyer, so with the seller; as with the lender, so with the borrower; as with the creditor, so with the debtor." Isaiah 24:1, 2

We tend to rely on wealth to provide our security, but here it says the contrary. The master and the servant will be in the same situation, as will the lender be in the same condition as the borrower.

"*3The land shall be entirely emptied and utterly plundered, for the LORD has spoken this word. 4The earth mourns and fades away, the world languishes and fades away; the haughty people of the earth languish. 5The earth is also defiled under its inhabitants, because they have transgressed the laws, changed the ordinance, broken the everlasting covenant. 6Therefore the curse has devoured the earth, and those who dwell in it are desolate. Therefore the inhabitants of the earth are burned, and few men are left." Isaiah 24:3-6*

Reasons why mankind will experience these calamities:

- It transgressed the law
- It distorted the truth (committed injustice)
- It broke the covenant

God warned Noah that anyone who sheds human blood will also suffer the same fate. They, however, transgressed the law, distorted the truth, and broke the covenant. They changed the pattern of life that God established and disturbed the family, which begins with God. (The woman should submit to the man, the man to Christ, and Christ to the Father.) They also broke the eternal covenant that Jesus made with us. When we break that covenant, we must pay the consequences and assume judgment. That is why we have commotion, a shaking, and bloodshed in every nation of the Earth.

"²⁰The earth shall reel to and fro like a drunkard, and shall totter like a hut; its transgression shall be heavy upon it, and it will fall, and not rise again." Isaiah 24:20

The climax of this passage is the establishment of God's Kingdom on Earth, with Jerusalem as its capital. For this to happen, everything described in Isaiah must first take place. Let us pray for the fulfillment of Isaiah 24 and for His Kingdom to come.

What causes this shaking or trembling?

"¹⁶For all that is in the world—the lust of the flesh, the lust of the eyes, and the pride of life—is not of the Father but is of the world. ¹⁷And the world is passing away, and the lust of it; but he who does the will of God abides forever." 1 John 2:16, 17

The main cause of the degeneration of the human character is pride. We should ask the Holy Spirit to show us the areas in which we have pride and to help us get rid of it. Humility is a decision not a feeling, as is pride. If we are prideful, it is because we have decided to be that way. In which case, we need to remember that pride is the thing God hates most. Dangerous and difficult times are quickly approaching; thus, we need to deal with our pride now before things get tougher.

Illustration: Take an apple or another fruit and put it in the refrigerator. Its corruption will slow down, but it will, nonetheless, occur without any possibility for reversal.

 codes

*Corruption is irreversible. It may slow down for a while
but it will be never be reversed.*

codes

"*17Therefore, if anyone is in Christ, he is a new creation; old
things have passed away; behold, all things have become new.*"
2 Corinthians 5:17

God is very realistic regarding this. He has never tried to
reverse corruption. He made a new creature through the
new birth—a new beginning without elements of corrupt-
tion therein.

"*1But know this, that in the last days perilous times will come:
2For men will be lovers of themselves, lovers of money, boasters,
proud, blasphemers, disobedient to parents, unthankful, unholy,
3unloving, unforgiving, slanderers, without self-control, brutal,
despisers of good, 4traitors, headstrong, haughty, lovers of pleasure
rather than lovers of God.*" 2 Timothy 3:1-4

This list contains 18 character immoralities. All are present in society today and are quickly increasing. There are
three characteristics, however, that make up the root of all
sins and of the corruption of man; most of our countries
are dominated by these three sins.

- Love of Self (ego)
- Love of money
- Love of pleasures

* **Love of the ego**

This is what drags society towards destruction because it causes mankind to say, "No one will do anything for me", "I am so important, that I cannot live with other people", or "No one can do things the way I do them." When two married people have irreconcilable differences, it is due to an exaggerated self-love that does not allow them to see things from the other person's perspective. Their concern with their individual needs and desires are placed above mutual benefit, the relaionship, or the covenant they made. They live in a constant, "I am important. Love me. I am first."

* **Love of money**

This is the powerful spirit that dominates modern society. Cultural thought today says that if something produces money it is justified in any of its actions. A clear example of this is the pornography industry which produces billions of dollars. It is impossible for righteousness to prevail when the love of money dominates us. Rich people always get their way.

* **Love of pleasures**

"4... lovers of pleasure rather than lovers of God, having a form of godliness but denying its power. And from such people turn away!" 2 Timothy 3:4, 5

"If it feels good, do it!" Many live by this motto without realizing it is leading them to destruction.

The Word says that many have "...a form of godliness..." This is a form of false Christianity because it denies God's supernatural power to change people. Today we no longer call homosexuality a sin; rather, we call it a lifestyle or a disorder. We no longer try to change homosexuals; instead, we conform and accept their manner of living as normal. The Church has lost its faith to see people change and have invented ways to coexist with sin. Paul says "....from such people turn away." "Such people" are those that do not want to change. We invest a lot of time at church in counseling and teaching people so they can be encouraged to change, but if they refuse, there is nothing more we can do but to avoid them.

What is the spiritual force behind all this?

"⁸Now as Jannes and Jambres resisted Moses, so do these also resist the truth: men of corrupt minds, disapproved concerning the faith." 2 Timothy 3:8

Behind the corruption of human nature is the subtle and deceitful spirit of the occult which accelerates corruption. Every time we find a continual and prolonged problem in a person or in a home, there is an occultist spirit at work.

What is the remedy?

"¹⁶All Scripture is given by inspiration of God, and is profitable for doctrine, for reproof, for correction, for instruction in righteousness, ¹⁷that the man of God may be complete, thoroughly equipped for every good work." 2 Timothy 3:16, 17

There is a weapon that can thoroughly equip us for every good work and help us to fight against the occultist spirit and corruption: The Word of God.

What is the end?

"¹I charge you therefore before God and the Lord Jesus Christ, who will judge the living and the dead at[a] His appearing and His kingdom: ²Preach the word! Be ready in season and out of season. Convince, rebuke, exhort, with all longsuffering and teaching."
2 Timothy 4:1, 2

Jesus is the Savior and the Judge, and preaching the Word is the strategy and the weapon—God's sword will destroy the work of the enemy.

God's judgment is a reality that occurs when mankind's rebellion and the degradation of his character defy the will of God. Sooner or later His judgment comes to remove us from evil and keep us from being lost forever. Our house should be built on the rock that is Christ Jesus. He saves those that believe in Him and judges the rest. The world is being shaken in every area, and everything that is not built on the Rock will be removed to establish the only unmovable, unshakeable Kingdom that exists: God's Kingdom.

The reason for this shaking is the degeneration of the human character which stems from the root of pride, producing an irreversible corruption. Only the power of God can kill the ego and create a new man in Christ's image.

Are you built on the Rock? Do you have anything to repent of? Have you preferred your ego, money, or the pleasures of this world over God's will? Is your life being shaken because God wants you to be built on the Cornerstone that is Jesus? We must decide to die to our self-sufficient ego that does not depend on God or His grace. We must be born to the new Self and carry our cross. Today is the time to submit our will to God's will so that we are not moved along with those things built on shifting ground.

In summary, we can say that:

* God is a God of judgment and of love.

* There are three eternal works that the Holy Spirit does on Earth. He convicts the world of sin, righteousness, and of judgment.

* God's judgment comes in three stages: preliminary, intermediate, and final.

* Doing the will of God does not exempt us from going through storms. The radical difference is that our house is built on the Rock that is Jesus Christ.

* Other things that can be shaken are one's personal life, every divided house, the system, businesses and large corporations, governments, religious institutions, physical structures and buildings, the heavens, and the Earth.

* The only thing that will remain unshakable is the Kingdom of God.

* The three main reasons why corruption comes to human beings are for transgressing laws, distorting the truth, committing injustice or breaking the covenant.

* The cause or root of this shaking is the degeneration of the human character which is caused by pride.

* The root of all sin and of the corruption of mankind is the love of ego, money, and pleasures.

* The force operating behind corruption is occultism.

* The escape route to all of this is to die to the ego, submit to the will of God, and to preach the Gospel.

CHAPTER V

ન્છન્છન્છ

How to Have Peace
in the Midst
of the Crisis

ન્છન્છન્છ

Throughout history, peace has been, and continues to be, one of the most important ingredients a person needs to be happy and feel satisfied on the inside. However, the world has a mistaken notion of what true peace is. They confuse it with tranquility or with the absence of aggression.

When reading the Word, we see that the peace of the world is different to God's peace. The world's peace is based on external circumstances. If a person has money, position, fame, or prestige, then he or she has peace. However, if something is lost, desperation and stress will immediately set in. This means that the peace that the world has is temporal and superficial. A serene and stable mind is not enough to overcome difficulties. There are thousands of people around the world right now that are upset because they lost their money, house, loved one, marriage, or something important. Their peace was based on what they had; therefore, it was lost when the crisis hit.

The peace of God comes to our heart and does not depend on external circumstances.

"27Peace I leave with you, My peace I give to you; not as the world gives do I give to you. Let not your heart be troubled, neither let it be afraid." John 14:27

We will study what biblical peace is, as it has several definitions. Let's begin by discarding what peace is *not*.

What is *not* peace?

True peace is not simply tranquility, stillness, or rest. These are the fruits, or the results, of peace. Peace is not the end of hostility. It is not a time without battles or the absence of war. If aggression against a person ceases but the relationship remains broken, then there is no true peace. When the word *peace* is used today, it is easy to understand what people are referring to. If there is no aggression, there is peace. However, if it were so limited, its meaning would be poor. Every divine virtue has the capacity to transform lives, and peace is a virtue of the heavenly Father's character.

God is not satisfied with the mere fact that mankind abstains from attacking each other. Rather, His idea of peace is for people to embrace, reconcile, and love one another once again; that the relationship becomes stronger than it was before it was broken. This truly entails more a ceasefire or to simply to end a war.

What is biblical peace?

In the Old Testament, the Hebrew word *shalom* is used, and the New Testament uses the Greek work *eirene*. Biblical peace is to mend or restore a broken relationship that became hostile. We can illustrate this idea with the figure of two people who hate each other and then make peace and reconcile. They put down their weapons, race towards each other's arms, and take up their relationship again. We then can say that said relationship was mended or restored to its original state and is stronger than before.

ৡৡৡ

The supreme need of every human being is
to be at peace with God.

ৡ ৡৡ

Christian peace is to love each other through unity, an alliance through which the brethren mutually love each other as they love themselves and God. Biblical peace is related to reconciliation, which is also the ministry we received from Jesus—to make peace between God and man.

"[18]Now all things are of God, who has reconciled us to Himself through Jesus Christ, and has given us the ministry of reconciliation." 2 Corinthians 5:18

What is our role as children of peace?

The children of peace are God's mature children who serve to foster reconciliation, as divine instruments of broken relationships between God and mankind. They are ambassadors of the Kingdom of God that reconcile the human race with the Heavenly Father. A good Christian brings reconciliation between God and his neighbor, between parents and children, and between families and marriages. A good Christian is one that repairs broken relationships.

"[20]Now then, we are ambassadors for Christ, as though God were pleading through us: we implore you on Christ's behalf, be reconciled to God." 2 Corinthians 5:20

At the time when the New Testament was written, the word *eirene* was used by the medical profession to describe the restoration of a broken bone. When both sides of the bone are joined until they calcify, the bone becomes stronger than it was originally. In fact, from then on, the spot where the fracture occurred is where the bone is least likely to ever break again. Therefore, the fracture site will later become the bone's strongest part. That happens when the bone heals correctly. In those times, when the bone was completely repaired, it was said to be *eirene*, or at peace.

Nowadays, an innumerable amount of people lack peace, tranquility, calm, or rest due to the problems they face. Beyond that, they live in the midst of broken relationships. The greatest difficulties present themselves between parents and children, husbands and wives, pastors and church members, and boyfriends and girlfriends. That is truly the main cause of the loss of the fruit of peace we previously mentioned. If that is your case, while you read this book God can intervene in a supernatural way to mend those relationships, so that you may again have peace with your loved ones.

What are the three dimensions of biblical peace?

Peace must be considered in terms of the heart. It is an internal, essential, and vital unity. It is a matter of love. In order for a person to be satisfied and complete in life, he or she needs to have peace in three dimensions, i.e., peace with God, self-peace, and peace with others.

1. Peace with God

"²⁰And by Him to reconcile all things to Himself, by Him, whether things on earth or things in heaven, having made peace through the blood of His cross. ²¹And you, who once were alienated and enemies in your mind by wicked works, yet now He has reconciled." Colossians 1:20, 21

We were enemies of God. All of us have sinned and broken our relationship with Him, for Adam bore the seed of our lives when he disobeyed. Adam's sin separated us from God, but Jesus' death on the cross mended that relationship and reconciled mankind to God. Jesus is the supreme peacemaker, who gave His life for us be at peace with the Father once again.

Mankind lives in continual enmity with God—man is guilty, while God is completely holy. Yet, it was He who took the initiative to mend and restore the relationship with us. After Adam's disobedience, God asked him, "Where are you?" What He was saying was, "My heart is broken for not having you as My child and friend. I will make a way so that we can be at peace. I will send My Son to die for your sins and His blood will reconcile us." Therein lays the essence of our discussion. Christ is our peace, and the fullness of it is found in Him.

Jesus also established peace between Jews and gentiles and between both peoples and God.

"¹⁵Having abolished in His flesh the enmity, that is, the law of commandments contained in ordinances, so as to create in

Himself one new man from the two, thus making peace, [16]and that He might reconcile them both to God in one body through the cross, thereby putting to death the enmity."
Ephesians 2:15, 16

Jesus had to die to restore the relationship between God and man. His main concern was not only to save mankind, forgive their sin, and keep them from going to hell. His purpose was to take them to a once-again intimate relationship with God, for them to recognize Him as their Father and Him to recognize them as His children.

How did God the Father make peace with mankind?

"[20]And by Him to reconcile all things to Himself, by Him, whether things on earth or things in heaven, having made peace through the blood of His cross." Colossians 1:20

He made peace through the blood of Jesus shed on the cross. The relationship through innocence that Adam enjoyed with God is not the same as the one we enjoy by grace because, after restoration, our relationship is stronger and unbreakable. It is *eirene*.

ɷɷɷ

My relationship with God is stronger through grace
than the one that Adam had through innocence.

ɷɷɷ

In Adam, the relationship was broken due to disobedience, but in Christ, it was mended by the supreme obedience of His death on the Cross. Through grace, it is now unbreakable and no one can separate us from Him.

"[37] Yet in all these things we are more than conquerors through Him who loved us. [38] For I am persuaded that neither death nor life, nor angels nor principalities nor powers, nor things present nor things to come, [39] nor height nor depth, nor any other created thing, shall be able to separate us from the love of God which is in Christ Jesus our Lord." Romans 8:37-39

Peace with God is based on Jesus, who now makes us unseparable from His love. The most important peace for mankind to have is peace with God, as it restores us to a close relationship with Him. That is where the difference from religion stems from. No religion can fill mankind with true divine peace. If we do not have peace with God, we cannot have peace with ourselves or with others. Neither can we have calm, tranquility, or rest, but rather it causes us a continual internal agitation, one that we transfer to every relationship and activity. It keeps human beings from ever reaching happiness.

What is mankind's spiritual condition?

"[1] And you He made alive, who were dead in trespasses and sins, [2] in which you once walked according to the course of this world, according to the prince of the power of the air, the spirit who now works in the sons of disobedience." Ephesians 2:1, 2

Because he lives in sin, man lacks an intimate relationship with God. Men and women are dissatisfied, empty, restless, and unhappy because their relationship with God is broken. Nowadays, there are people with no peace because they lost material things, were affected by the financial crisis, or were struck with a personal crisis. However, it is not by coincidence that you are reading this book. God desires to reconcile you to Himself. He wants to mend and restore that broken relationship, and it has already been done through Jesus Christ! He took the initiative! The only things we need to do are draw near and say, "Yes. I accept reconciliation with You. I accept our having a relationship again."

"*19I create the fruit of the lips: 'Peace, peace to him who is far off and to him who is near,' Says the LORD, 'And I will heal him.' 20But the wicked are like the troubled sea, When it cannot rest, whose waters cast up mire and dirt. 21'There is no peace,' Says my God, 'for the wicked.'" Isaiah 57:19-21*

What has God taught us in these verses? People who lack a relationship with Him are like the troubled waters of the sea; they are never still and, due to much restlessness, cast up dirt, mire, impurities, and choppy water. They are double-minded people. Why is the sea always restless? Why does the ocean get turbulent? This gives the image of a man that has separated from God, and whose trust is in the world and its objects. People have trusted in their self-sufficiency, material goods, possessions, prestige, and wealth. However, when they go to sleep, they have no peace because they have enmity with God.

The consequences of not having peace with God are:

- The person who has no peace with God cannot make good decisions.

"⁵I am the vine, you are the branches. He who abides in Me, and I in him, bears much fruit; for without Me you can do nothing." John 15:5

- The person who does not have peace with God cannot be at peace with himself or with others.

"¹⁹I create the fruit of the lips: 'Peace, peace to him who is far off and to him who is near,' Says the LORD, 'And I will heal him.'" Isaiah 57:19

- The person who has no peace with God disturbs those around him. However, if he is at peace with God, he will be at peace even with his enemies.

"⁷When a man's ways please the LORD, He makes even his enemies to be at peace with him." Proverbs 16:7

- The person who doesn't have peace with God will never achieve what he desires, His ways are uncertain because only God knows how to give him what he yearns for.

"¹¹For I know the thoughts that I think toward you, says the LORD, thoughts of peace and not of evil, to give you a future and a hope." Jeremiah 29:11

- The thoughts of people who have no peace with God are erratic and saturated with negativity, pessimism, depression, etc. However, the peace of God guards your mind.

"7And the peace of God, which surpasses all understanding, will guard your hearts and minds through Christ Jesus." Philippians 4:7

What are the solutions or escapes which people seek to calm that lack of peace?

People are never satisfied. In their constant state of turmoil, worry, and lack of peace they are unsuccessful in finding satisfaction in anything they do or have. Nothing fills their souls, and that leads them to seek other things to fill the void and calm their anxiety. *Pleasure* and *wrong motivations* are the escapes people seek in their ignorance to calm their lack of peace.

• **Pleasure**

People try to escape their lack of peace through situations that produce pleasure or provide an escape, even if it is brief. That is why they travel, play sports, give themselves to illicit sex and immorality, try to obtain higher social, economic, or employment positions, pursue fame, money, or prestige, abuse alcohol, consume drugs, or take refuge in a religion or therapeutic exercise.

Do we not see this day after day? Has the world ever been as restless as it is today? Observe how determined people are to seek pleasure. Many live looking for their pleasure fix to quiet their inner desperation. The world demands new forms of entertainment, and seeks increasingly intense emotions to feel stimulated and find meaning in life. They stuff themselves with movies, theater, music, and more.

♦ **Wrong motivation**

Human beings are motivated to live and to do things for different reasons. In the case of believers, our motivations should be love, fear of the Lord, doing His will, and not pleasing ourselves. However, the motivation of those who do not know the Lord is to please themselves and seek their own satisfaction. This leads them to fall in to a greater void and keeps them from having peace in their heart.

A person without peace is unstable, like ocean waves

Why does the ocean have waves, tides, and water currents? Scientists say that it is due to the ocean constantly reacting to two opposing forces:

· **The moon's pull**. It partially controls the sand and the ocean's movement.

· **The magnetic pull from the center of the Earth.** This is a very strong magnetic force that pulls opposite to the moon's pull.

The moon's influence and the Earth's magnetic pull struggle in opposite directions. This is one of the causes of the ocean's constant movement. The tide, the water currents, and the winds that blow over the ocean, in addition to the influences of the sun and the moon, create large and small movements. These movements can become large storms, swells, and even tidal waves like the tsunami that struck the coast of Thailand in 2006. In the ocean of our life, we will also experience opposing forces. On one side, modern man is pulled by the enemy and his forces—desire of the world, lust of the flesh, lust of the eyes, love of money, greed, covetousness, immorality, the need to satisfy loneliness and rejection, etc. On the other hand, God calls him to seek the Kingdom and its righteousness because God loves him and wants to provide him with peace. Man needs to be at peace with God for his soul to find rest; otherwise, he will never be satisfied.

All of this is an expression of the fundamental restlessness of human beings that, without God, develops into the illness: lack of peace or lack of rest. Man lives in sin. He is unstable, does not know mental or spiritual peace, and doesn't have peace in his heart. James says that such a man is double-minded and, like the waves of the sea, goes to and fro, back and forth, and back again.

"⁶But let him ask in faith, with no doubting, for he who doubts is like a wave of the sea driven and tossed by the wind." James 1:6

Man feels that he should do what is right, but likes to do wrong, what's inconvenient to him. That is where he finds himself pulled by two extremes. His life and his ways are then like the waves of the sea that never finds serenity. He finds himself pulled by different sins. He knows he should respect his marriage, spend time with his children, be honest, and serve God. Though he knows what is right, he is unsuccessful in doing so. He has an inner struggle because he is caught between two waters, and that impedes him from being at peace with himself.

What is the solution that Jesus provides us?

"³¹Therefore do not worry, saying, 'What shall we eat?' or 'What shall we drink?' or 'What shall we wear?' ³²For after all these things the Gentiles seek. For your heavenly Father knows that you need all these things. ³³But seek first the kingdom of God and His righteousness, and all these things shall be added to you." Matthew 6:31-33

Jesus counsels us not to be anxious or worried, or to get filled with insecurity, fear, or restlessness. The Father knows we have needs, and He provides us the solution. It is to seek His Kingdom and its righteousness. When we do so, everything is added on to us; material things, what we need, and even what we simply like and want to have.

Do you need to make peace with God? Are you burdened, full of tribulation, or disturbed by problems and the current crisis? Do you feel insecure and dissatisfied? Are you looking for something to motivate you to live? Are you weighed down by family or financial problems? Read the solution to your lack of peace:

"28Come to Me, all you who labor and are heavy laden, and I will give you rest. 29Take My yoke upon you and learn from Me, for I am gentle and lowly in heart, and you will find rest for your souls. 30For My yoke is easy and My burden is light." Matthew 11:28-30

When we have peace with God we are reconciled with the Father and our broken relationships are restored. He fulfills His promise to give us peace. Let's give Him our burdens and our problems. You and I lack the strength to solve them. There are certain things that we cannot explain or understand, and others that are beyond our control. What must we do? Simply give them over to God and trust that He will perform a miracle and put peace in our heart.

2. Peace with ourselves

"1Therefore, having been justified by faith, we have peace with God through our Lord Jesus Christ." Romans 5:1

Peace must be made through Jesus Christ. Only then will we have peace with ourselves. Do you have peace with God? Can you sleep well at night? Do you have peace in the midst of the storm? Have you received the Prince of Peace in your heart? You will not have peace with yourself if you do not first mend your relationship with God, which was broken by sin, iniquity, and our independence of Him. Jesus reconciled us and, by faith, we can lay claim, recognize, and receive that peace. When Jesus forgives our sin and the Father gives us identity as His children, we find peace and meaning in life.

Testimony: Yocasta had been unemployed for six months and her husband for three. They remained at peace, trusting in the Lord and in His provision. One day, the pastor made an altar call for people who do not have a job and he prayed for both of them. Five minutes later, Yocasta received a call with a job offer! The following week, her husband was called back to the job he had lost!

3. Peace with others

"9Blessed are the peacemakers, for they shall be called sons of God." Matthew 5:9

In the Greek, the word son is the word *juois*, which means a *mature son*. Peacemakers are Christians that promote peace, reconciliation, and the mending and restoration of broken relationships between husbands and wives, parents and children, and other family members. They are ones that take the Gospel of Peace to their homes and neighborhoods.

Two of the main tenants of our vision are to *evangelize* and to *affirm* and one of the ways of doing so is through the *Houses of Peace*. Here, leaders are trained to be peacemakers, to take the peace of Jesus Christ to other homes, and to be the ambassadors of reconciliation to a world, society, or neighborhood that lacks peace. This is one of the ways our church and our vision restore peace to the city. They are called Houses of Peace because, in them, broken relationships are restored. They foster calm, tranquility, rest, and biblical peace to the neighborhood and the city.

"[15]*And how shall they preach unless they are sent? As it is written: 'How beautiful are the feet of those who preach the gospel of peace, Who bring glad tidings of good things!'"* Romans 10:15

Each leader of a House of Peace is an ambassador of the Kingdom, and brings peace to human beings that are separated from their relationship to God. That is why the Bible calls them blessed because they are the carriers of the good news of salvation, healing, prosperity, and above all, reconciliation and restoration. They are the ones called to mend the relationship between God and mankind and amongst mankind itself. Are you willing to go to a world that has no peace? Are you willing to take the Gospel of peace? Are you willing to be a carrier of peace? Can we have peace with others? Are you a mature child, a peacemaker?

"[18]*If it is possible, as much as depends on you, live peaceably with all men."* Romans 12:18

Every one of us should do everything possible to mend broken relationships, reconcile people to God, and reunite them to their families.

Illustration: Do you have a broken relationship? Is there a broken bone in your family, church, job, office, or school? Are you a mature son or daughter? Are you willing to mend and correct that relationship?

When David met his brave men, he set a key condition to see whether or not they would be part of his leadership team.

"¹⁷And David went out to meet them, and answered and said to them, 'If you have come peaceably to me to help me, my heart will be united with you; but if to betray me to my enemies, since there is no wrong in my hands, may the God of our fathers look and bring judgment.'" 1 Chronicles 12:17

"If you have come peaceably..." What David was saying was, "Are you the type of person that seeks peace or are you coming to cause me problems?" Expanding on that question we could say, "Are you coming to have a relationship with me and strengthen my leadership or do you come to weaken it? If you are coming to cause turbulence, fighting, or quarreling, I don't even want you on my team. In fact, if you are, may God judge you, or make you pay, no matter how talented or anointed you are. If, however, you come to love me and to be a peacemaker, then join the team." Are you a leader or part of a leadership team for personal ambition or to strengthen it?

Conclusion:

There are people all over the world right now that do not have peace with God, with man, or even with themselves. They go to bed dissatisfied, worried, restless, and insecure due to the economic crisis or to a personal crisis they are facing, to things beyond their control. They wake up every day with the same uncertainty and lack of direction. They don't know how to find a solution to the restlessness that troubles them like a turbulent sea on the inside.

Right now I would like to guide in prayer all the people reading this book who feel like the ones described. We know that there cannot be peace without knowing and restoring the relationship with God. If you have never known Christ as Lord and Savior of your life, do it now, because you cannot have peace unless it is through Jesus and have faith in His sacrifice on the cross. If you are going through a crisis which seems to be like a stormy sea, then repeat this prayer out loud with me.

"Heavenly Father, I recognize that I am a sinner and that I have disobeyed your laws and sinned against You. I repent of all my sins. I confess with my mouth that Jesus is the Son of God and I believe, with all my heart, that the Father raised Him from the dead. Lord, forgive my sins and give me Your peace. Today I recognize that Jesus died on the cross and, through His sacrifice and the shedding of His blood, He reconciled me to You. Give me Your peace and take away the restlessness and worries from my heart. I reconcile with myself and with others, and I commit to restore relationships that have been broken. I give you every burden and wound in my heart, in the name of Jesus. Thank you, Lord!

Points to remember:

- The supreme need of human beings is to have peace with God.

- Peace is not only calm or tranquility. Those are fruits of peace but not complete peace.

- Peace is not the absence of fighting, of war, or the ceasing of hostilities.

- Biblical peace is to mend a broken relationship and make it stronger than it was before.

- Biblical peace is the reconciliation between two people that previously hated each other but that now love one another.

- The three dimensions of peace are peace with God, peace with ourselves, and peace with others.

- Jesus is our peace because He reconciled us with the Father through His death.

- God not only wants to save mankind and to forgive his sins but He also wants them to have a close and an intimate relationship with them.

- Jesus made peace through His blood, which was shed at the Cross of Calvary.

- Mankind's spiritual condition is restlessness, worry, and lack of peace. Their life is like a tempestuous sea.

- As a result of their lack of peace, people seek pleasure, or something to motivate them, but always end up dissatisfied.

- We are called to be peacemakers.

CHAPTER VI

ಹಿ ಹಿ ಹಿ

Faith

Tested by Fire

ಹಿ ಹಿ ಹಿ

F or many years, the Church has been taught that trials come as the consequence of sin. When we experience hardship, people think it is an indication of sin in our life or perhaps that we are operating outside of God's will. This is a very dangerous concept, because based on this mentality, when anything goes wrong, we begin to ask if something is wrong with us or those around us.

The idea that we are not doing things right becomes recurring, often leading to the belief that we have sinned against God. If this were true, then Moses, David, and other heroes of the faith also lived in sin, for they went through great difficulties and overcame enormous obstacles to fulfill God's call. Most of God's people relate trials to challenges or sin. I want to correct this because it is not so. The Bible says:

"³Jesus answered, 'Neither this man nor his parents sinned, but that the works of God should be revealed in him.'" John 9:3

When we face a sickness or family tragedy, people criticize us asking, "Why did you have that miscarriage? Why did your house burn down? What are you doing wrong? Surely this must be due to sin in your life!" This is very common today, and it also happened in Jesus' time. Religious people concluded in the verse we just read that the man was blind due to sin, either his or his parents'. However, Jesus said that his blindness was, *"that the works of God should be revealed in him."*

What is the glory?

The word *glory* is the translation of the Greek word *doxa* and it means: the true and intrinsic nature of who God is in His totality, character, perfection, and attributes. There is also the Hebrew word *kabod* which means *weight*. Jesus said this problem came about to manifest God's nature. How can this adversity reveal God's nature? The word *nature* explains how something is. The question then should be, "How is God? How is the sound of His voice? How does He think? How does He feel? How is His character? How is His true nature?" The only way to know God is to receive the revelation of His glory. A person's physical strength can only be known when they lift up something heavy. You can say that you are strong, but only a test will reveal the truth. In order to know God's glory, we need the presence of a problem or challenge; a situation that requires a miracle.

∾∾∾

God will not be able to prove or manifest
His glory until we need a miracle.

∾∾∾

Being tested is not a demonic activity, for this is connected with the development of faith. Jesus said that God decided to show His power through the blind man, as miracles are a sign that a supernatural power is at work over a natural being. It is then when God's glory, power, and nature are revealed through the trial. Not only does God protect us in our problems but He also tests and reveals Himself through adversity.

Concepts we should understand when we go thorough problems, crises, or difficulties:

◆ **It is necessary to go through trials.**

"⁶In this you greatly rejoice, though now for a little while, if need be, you have been grieved by various trials." 1 Peter 1:6

◆ **Our faith must be tested that it may be trustworthy.**

"⁷That the genuineness of your faith, being much more precious than gold that perishes, though it is tested by fire, may be found to praise, honor, and glory at the revelation of Jesus Christ." 1 Peter 1:7

ৡৡৡ
Never trust anyone until they have been tested.
ৡৡৡ

◆ **At times, trials come due to disobedience.**

"¹⁵But let none of you suffer as a murderer, a thief, an evildoer, or as a busybody in other people's matters. ¹⁶Yet if anyone suffers as a Christian, let him not be ashamed, but let him glorify God in this matter." 1 Peter 4:15, 16

One thing is to suffer for being a liar, an evildoer, or for meddling in other people's matters, but it is another to go through trials that God permits—He does not send them; He only allows them—to test our faith. There are cases of people that go through problems because they sinned or as a consequence of their bad decisions; however, in most cases, trials come because they are part of the Christian's walk.

◆ **Trials are temporary and fleeting.**

"17For our light affliction, which is but for a moment, is working for us a far more exceeding and eternal weight of glory."
2 Corinthians 4:17

One lie of the enemy is to make people believe that trials will last forever or that they are the only ones going through them. The Word of God teaches that everyone will experience trials and tribulation, but they are temporary and passing.

Testimony: Luis went through a season of lack that lasted for a year and a half. It was tough because he would work and work yet not make a single dollar. Meanwhile, God always provided for him through his family and friends. After that time, he started a business with two people from church. After breakthrough prayers, they began to win contracts, each larger than the previous. Luis passed the test. He remained faithful and God returned to him what he had lost, and more.

◆ **We cannot be surprised when trials come.**

"12Beloved, do not think it strange concerning the fiery trial which is to try you, as though some strange thing happened to you." 1 Peter 4:12

There is a false teaching in modern Christianity that proclaims that, if we obey God, we will live problem free, our Christian walk will be a bed of roses, and everything will be perfectly fine. However, that is not what the Bible says. The Word of God teaches that we will enter the Kingdom of God with pressure and persecution; therefore, we must prepare, change our mentality, and be ready, knowing that trials will come.

ﾚﾚﾚ
Your faith is as strong as the trial you survive.
ﾚﾚﾚ

If you want to know how strong you are, just consider your measure of faith. For this, your faith must be tested; otherwise, you cannot determine your strength.

ﾚﾚﾚ
Faith that is not tested cannot be trusted.
ﾚﾚﾚ

There are a lot of people that go to church, dance, rejoice, and shout "Hallelujah!" All of that is good, but when God tries their faith, and they lose their job or something important in their life, they leave the church. What happened? Their faith was only a façade. They lacked a strong faith.

Why must our faith be tested by fire?

The key reason for being tested by fire is to weigh and reveal the motives and intentions for which we follow, seek, and serve God. What is your motive for calling Jesus Lord? What motivates you to seek Him? What motivates you to serve Him? Is it because He has blessed you or restored your marriage? Do you serve Him because He healed your body? Why do you serve God?

What is our motivation to serve God?

Next, let us look at the sixth chapter of the book of John, where Jesus challenges and reveals the hearts of many of His disciples to show them their motivation for following Him. Jesus explains in this passage that He is the True Bread that descended from Heaven. He declared that, from that moment on, they had to eat of His flesh and drink of His blood and thereby live through Him as He had lived through the Father. Of course, this is all spiritually symbolic. His purpose was no longer to tend to their needs or about feeding them the fish and the bread. It was about knowing that as His life flowed through them, they would in turn give it to the world. He also declared that the manna that fell in the desert was a miraculous provision from God to keep His people from dying of hunger. While they traversed the desert, He met their basic needs for food, drink, clothing, and shoes, and He did so miraculously for forty years. However, those days were over and the people now had to learn to eat the true Bread. Everyone had to learn to seek and follow Jesus, not for the benefits and the miracles but because He was God, the Messiah that had descended from Heaven. The disciples had to continually go to Him to obtain the true Bread which would serve to satisfy their needs and also enough to feed the hungry multitude.

❧❧❧

The motivations and intentions of our heart
will be tried by fire.

❧❧❧

"24When the people therefore saw that Jesus was not there, nor His disciples, they also got into boats and came to Capernaum, seeking Jesus." John 6:24

The people sought Him because they knew that He gave free breakfast, lunch, and dinner. Today, many follow Jesus because He pays their mortgage, heals their body, restores their marriage, and delivers them from depression.

"²⁵And when they found Him on the other side of the sea, they said to Him, 'Rabbi, when did You come here?' ²⁶Jesus answered them and said, 'Most assuredly, I say to you, you seek Me, not because you saw the signs, but because you ate of the loaves and were filled.'"
John 6:25, 26

Again, many seek Jesus for the blessings He can give and not for who He is.

"²⁸Then they said to Him, 'What shall we do, that we may work the works of God?' ²⁹Jesus answered and said to them, 'This is the work of God, that you believe in Him whom He sent." John 6:28, 29

Jesus tells them, "Do not believe in Me because I gave you fish and bread. Don't put your faith in material things. Believe in Me because I am God." Have you asked yourself why you serve, follow, and obey Him? Jesus is changing your motivation and your faith from material things—food, drink, and blessings—to Him, because He is the true Bread of life.

"³⁰Therefore they said to Him, 'What sign will You perform then, that we may see it and believe You? What work will You do? ³¹Our fathers ate the manna in the desert; as it is written, 'He gave them bread from heaven to eat.' ³²Then Jesus said to them, 'Most assuredly, I say to you, Moses did not give you the bread from heaven, but My Father gives you the true bread from heaven.'" John 6:30-33

They said their fathers followed Moses for the miracles He performed. Likewise, there are many today who follow Jesus only for the house or car He gave them, and that proves the motivation of their heart. What happens, however, when they lose it? Do they continue to serve Him? Do they continue in His ways? Do they continue being His disciples?

"34Then they said to Him, 'Lord, give us this bread always.'"
John 6:34

We must choose from two types of bread—perishable bread or the true Bread of Heaven that is Jesus. Are you following a particular ministry? Is your faith in Jesus or in natural blessings?

Illustration: If there is someone that should have left the ministry, it is me. I have been persecuted and criticized, in and out of church, both in this country and in others. I have been rejected by pastors. I have been stolen from and lied to. They have even put my image on the front page of newspapers and have printed falsehoods about me. However, I am still standing. After walking with Jesus for 22 years, clearly my faith has been put to the test.

Don't tell me that problems or temptations can cause you to throw away what you have learned, in twenty years, from one day to the next. If so, where is your faith? Is it in God or on the things that God gives? Let us remember the time when Jesus was in the boat with His disciples and a storm arose. He could have avoided it but did not because He wanted to test the faith of His disciples. Jesus went to sleep to see how they would react. When He awoke, the storm did not immediately subside. Instead, He asked the disciples, "Where is your faith?" Their faith was being tested by fire. How wonderful to know that the Prince of Peace was with them in the midst of the storm! That is the same word I give to those that are going thorough storms, "Live in peace in the midst of the storm because the Prince of Peace is with you."

Jesus essentially said, "You say that you are My disciple and that I am your God, so then let me sleep." He allowed the storm to come—He did not cause it, but He allowed it—to test the faith of His disciples. The Bible says we will not get a test greater than what we can stand. Therefore, if you are going through a storm, it is because you can overcome it in the name of Jesus. The test will equal your measure of faith. If your trial is a big one, it is because that is how much God thinks of your faith.

ෙෙෙ

The greater the trial the greater the faith.

ෙෙෙ

There are people who cannot survive the trial. That is sad because if they cannot survive it, it means they cannot survive success either. Their faith will not be ready for it. They would forget God. He tries us first with a little and, if we are faithful, He gives us more. After we are tested, He gives us success. Sometimes we think that God does not answer our prayers because He denies us what we have asked for, but that is not the case. A "no" is also an answer from God because He knows what is best for us.

Illustration: If your ten-year-old child asks for the keys to your car, you would say, "No". Why? It is because you know that a child is not capable of driving a car, and you want to protect him. He does not have the necessary size, maturity, or knowledge to do it well. God does the same with His children.

"⁵¹I am the living bread which came down from heaven. If anyone eats of this bread, he will live forever; and the bread that I shall give is My flesh, which I shall give for the life of the world. ⁵²The Jews therefore quarreled among themselves, saying, 'How can this Man give us His flesh to eat?' ⁵³Then Jesus said to them, 'Most assuredly, I

say to you, unless you eat the flesh of the Son of Man and drink His blood, you have no life in you.'" John 6:51-53

This is what angered the disciples and the multitude. They did not understand what He was referring to regarding their eating of His flesh and drinking of His blood. What does that imply? It implies a total commitment to God. It is to drink Jesus in the morning, afternoon, and evening. It is to obey, commit, yield, and give yourself completely to Him. That is what eating and drinking Jesus is about. However, many today are equally offended by that because they don't want to lose their life. They don't want to commit.

❧❧❧

*Their commitment in times of crisis reveals
the heart of those that are next to us.*

❧❧❧

"60Therefore many of His disciples, when they heard this, said, 'This is a hard saying; who can understand it?' 61When Jesus knew in Himself that His disciples complained about this, He said to them, 'Does this offend you?'" John 6:60, 61

Jesus asks, "Are you one of those people who gets angry and no longer serves God when you lose your job? Are you one of those people that get upset and leave the church when they ask for your commitment to the vision? Are you one of those disciples that drop everything and run away when they ask you to evangelize or to pray? Are you one of the ones that stop serving God when you lose your house? Jesus takes away the gifts because He wants to give us the One that grants the blessings. The question is "Where is your faith?" What is it placed on? Is it on your job, talent, or abilities? Is it on the Church or is it placed on God? Your faith cannot be based on what people from this or other ministries are doing. Many people will disappoint you. Do not depend on people's behavior, but rather depend on God. You are not here just for the fish and the bread; you are here to give others the bread of life. We have to get away from the mentality that we go to church solely to have our needs met. Jesus does not want us to seek only that. Instead, He wants us to seek Him because He is the true Bread of life that feed us and others.

"66From that time many of His disciples went back and walked with Him no more. 67Then Jesus said to the twelve, 'Do you also want to go away?'"John 6:66, 67

Many turned back, or walked away, including some that were His disciples. Here we learn an important principle.

ॐॐॐ
*People think if they leave, you will be worth less
or that you will end up falling apart.*
ॐॐॐ

People try to use this as a weapon of manipulation. For example, in a church, the accountant, administrator, music leader, sound technician, or musician says, "If I leave this place, they will not be able to function. This would fall apart without me."

What was Jesus' response? He told them, "Whoever wants to go, just leave!" He told the twelve, including Peter. "Do you also want to go?" Jesus was saying, "I don't want you with Me for the fish and the bread. I want you by My side for My flesh and blood, because you are committed to Me, to the Kingdom, and to the vision." They replied, "If You do not bless us, we will not follow You." In other words, their faith was as strong as the fish and the bread they ate. However, Peter said a great truth,

"⁶⁸But Simon Peter answered Him, 'Lord, to whom shall we go? You have the words of eternal life.'" Juan 6:68

Who can separate us from the love of God? Can a meal, job, relationship, free sandwich, or illicit affair? Nothing can separate us from the love of God! Many people will criticize you when you are going through storms, but those who criticize you don't even have a God to go to. Our faith should be placed on our heavenly Father because, when people go through storms, they will seek you and your God for help, as there is no one else to look to for anything real.

"⁶⁹Also we have come to believe and know that You are the Christ, the Son of the living God." John 6:69

♦ **The key is to persevere and continue.**

Note that Peter changed from being a seeker of material rewards, fish, and bread to being a disciple that believed and followed Jesus. We all need to undergo that change: to not only seek, follow, and serve God for what He gives us, but rather for whom He is. Jesus walked this Earth in faith, despite being betrayed by Judas, one of His twelve, one of His closest. However, Jesus persevered and continued. It does not matter who surrounds us, how much we have suffered, how much they rejected us, and how much they spoke negatively of us and persecuted us, we must persevere and continue. Jesus said, "The Father gave me a task to do and I will complete it." Don't let people separate you from the work that the Father gave you to do. Do not stray from the vision, the purpose, or the will of God because that is more important than all other things. Judas ended up committing suicide but Jesus persevered and continued.

What held Jesus back? Did the suicide of his friend and personal disciple do so? Of course not! It hurt Him a lot, but He did not allow that to stop Him. If He had, you and I would not have salvation today. Perhaps people blamed Him and said, "You are responsible for Judas' death." However, Jesus must have answered, "He chose His own death." Jesus then persevered and continued.

ॐॐॐ

*Everything that holds you back
marks the measure of your faith.*

ॐॐॐ

What things are holding you back in life at this very moment? Is it a marriage, financial, or health problem? What is slowing you down? You cannot allow anything to hold you back. You must continue and do the works of God. One day, Ministerio El Rey Jesus (King Jesus Ministry) will go on without me, my wife, and without other people because if God was the one that established it, then it will remain. God's work must continue and be fulfilled.

Illustration: I had certain leaders that walked alongside me, that sowed and worked hard but, when the pressure of the work, service, vision, and trials came, they were unable to stand it and left. They were key people in the ministry. Though they were strong pillars, even ministers, they decided to leave. However I persevered and continued because I must finish God's work.

There are many that still live in the past. But that past has held them back from serving God and from doing His will. Someone hurt you, betrayed you, or spoke ill of you. Perhaps your husband was unfaithful. If you are a pastor, perhaps it was a church member or an important leader who hurt you and left. Whatever the case may be, you must persevere and continue.

Some consider themselves so important and indispensable that they think that, if they leave, the church would come to a standstill. However, they would be surprised because God always has someone else to occupy their place. We are all important, but no one is indispensable in the Body of Christ. Therefore, with or without you, and with or without me, the work of God must persevere and continue.

I have learned not to cling to people. I love and appreciate them and always affirm them as a spiritual father. I give them self-esteem and identity, and raise them up and believe in them. Yet, I have understood that nothing is eternal, and that one day they will no longer be with me. One day they will leave and make a life for themselves. Therefore, I should be ready for that and be sure to complete my share of God's work. I must persevere and continue.

How does God measure success?

ॐॐॐ
*Success is measured by the ability to
maintain a personal balance in times of crisis.*
ॐॐॐ

There are people that turn into putty, fall apart, and even get nervous breakdowns and phobia attacks whenever a problem or a crisis arises.

Illustration: A grave problem surfaced in a United States university. As a result, one of the professors that taught there suffered a nervous breakdown and practically lost his mind. That person did not have a personal balance because his life was not founded on Jesus Christ. The crisis came and knocked him down.

❧❧❧
*Maturity is the ability to deal with
the expected and the unexpected.*
❧❧❧

Because of this, I realized from the beginning that trials should be expected because they will come and are necessary. For that which we cannot anticipate, we must be prepared, trusting always in Christ, the Rock, unmovable through the ages. Despite what may come, we must persevere and continue.

I will tell you how mature you are when I see you under pressure. It doesn't matter how much you talk, dance, shout, or state and proclaim that you are a strong and spiritual man. In times of pressure the truth comes out.

❧❧❧
*The way you respond to tragedy
marks the measure of your maturity.*
❧❧❧

Illustration: I was preparing for a miracle crusade in El Salvador when, suddenly, I received a call informing me that one of my sisters had suffered a massive heart attack and had died instantly. That very night I was to preach at the crusade. I went to the Lord in prayer with my heart aching because of the bad news and He reminded me of Jesus' words, "Let the dead bury the dead." He reminded me that my sister was not the priority but rather the will of God. I realize this sounds cruel to many people to hear, but it just as cruel and painful for Jesus to say it. I finished the miracle crusade and God did extraordinary things. Thousands were saved and healed. Other thousands entered into the Kingdom of God that night and their lives were transformed. I was able to do according to His will. It was tough. It was difficult. Though my heart was heavy, I had to continue to do God's work.

He will not keep painful situations from coming to our lives because, through them, He will form our character and bring our nature to light. Everything He allows is because He knows something about the future we don't. Therefore, we affirm once again that we must let God be God while we persevere and continue.

How tough is your trial? Can you continue to fight the good fight of faith?

A characteristic of the Kingdom of God is to show the world how strong His people are. God allows trials and difficulties. He allows us to go through suffering to show that He is God and that His Kingdom is unshakable and greater than the kingdom of the world.

ঌ৵ঌ৵ঌ৵

The greatest moments of your life
will come after the trials.

ঌ৵ঌ৵ঌ৵

"¹²Fight the good fight of faith, lay hold on eternal life, to which you were also called and have confessed the good confession in the presence of many witnesses." 1 Timothy 6:12

This battle is for your faith, and you must go through it under intense pressure. The devil wants to put out your faith. He wants to destroy it because it is the shield you use to put out all the fiery darts he sends your way.

Illustration: Imagine that you go to church today and you rejoice, praise God, and happily receive the message. Later, on your way home, you crash into another vehicle as you are driving. At that very moment the evil one's darts will come flying at you saying, "Where is your God? Didn't He say that He would send His angels to protect you?" Well, I ask you, "Will you continue to serve God even if you crashed your car? Will you continue to serve Jesus, as His disciple, even though He "supposedly" didn't protect you?

How did Job pass the test of his faith?

Let us study the life of a man in the Word of God that was righteous and perfect in all his ways, but still had to face a very difficult trial.

"⁶Now there was a day when the sons of God came to present themselves before the LORD, and Satan also came among them. ⁷And the LORD said to Satan, 'From where do you come?' So Satan answered the LORD and said, 'From going to and fro on the earth,

and from walking back and forth on it.' *⁸Then the LORD said to Satan, 'Have you considered My servant Job, that there is none like him on the earth, a blameless and upright man, one who fears God and shuns evil?' ⁹So Satan answered the LORD and said, 'Does Job fear God for nothing? ¹⁰Have You not made a hedge around him, around his household, and around all that he has on every side? You have blessed the work of his hands, and his possessions have increased in the land. ¹¹But now, stretch out Your hand and touch all that he has, and he will surely curse You to Your face."* Job 1:6-11

Satan challenged God to strip Job of everything to see if, after losing his precious family, flocks, livestock, and riches, he would not deny Him, still recognize Him as God, and continue to serve Him. God accepted that challenge.

"¹²And the LORD said to Satan, 'Behold, all that he has is in your power; only do not lay a hand on his person.' So Satan went out from the presence of the LORD." Job 1:12

I can imagine Satan accusing us before God, telling Him He has prospered us too much and given us a home, good family, great ministry, a nice job, and a great blessing. He challenges God by saying that we have not proved our love for Him. He tells God, "Touch him to see if he continues to serve You for what You give Him or because He really loves You. Test him!"

As soon as he received God's permission, Satan destroyed Job's family and his wealth. To make matters worse, while Job did nothing but resist and wait on God's salvation, instead of joining him to help, his wife told him the following.

"⁹Then his wife said to him, 'Do you still hold fast to your integrity? Curse God and die!' ¹⁰But he said to her, 'You speak as one of the foolish women speaks. Shall we indeed accept good from God, and

shall we not accept adversity?' In all this Job did not sin with his lips." Job 2:9, 10

"⁶Is not your reverence your confidence? And the integrity of your ways your hope?" Job 4:6

I imagine that Job turned around to face his wife and said, "I will not compromise my principles. I will not murmur or complain. I will not curse God, for I serve Him because I love Him, not for what He gave me." Despite it all, Job retained his integrity. We could go on to say much about Job but I want us to see how the story ends.

What was Job's end result?

"⁷... after the LORD had spoken these words to Job, that the LORD said to Eliphaz the Temanite, 'My wrath is aroused against you and your two friends, for you have not spoken of Me what is right, as My servant Job has. ⁸Now therefore, take for yourselves seven bulls and seven rams, go to My servant Job, and offer up for yourselves a burnt offering; and My servant Job shall pray for you. For I will accept him, lest I deal with you according to your folly; because you have not spoken of Me what is right, as My servant Job has.' ⁹So Eliphaz the Temanite and Bildad the Shuhite and Zophar the Naamathite went and did as the LORD commanded them; for the LORD had accepted Job." Job 42:7-9

This happens after Job had lost it all: his sheep, money, livestock, and family. His three friends spoke badly about him and accused him saying, "Look at what has happened to you. Wasn't God protecting you? Didn't God promise to supply for all your needs? Isn't God your healer?" Job, however, did not seek revenge against them, nor did he become offended. Instead, he prayed that God would forgive them. That is the advice for many of you. If your friends are saying, "Where is your God? If God is your provider, why did you lose your house? If He is your healer, why doesn't He heal you?" Do not criticize them. Pray for them that God may forgive them.

"10And the LORD restored Job's losses when he prayed for his friends. Indeed the LORD gave Jobs twice as much as he had before."
Job 42:10

Do you want God to bless you? Then pray for those who criticize and persecute you. Maintain a correct, forgiving attitude towards them. God will forgive them and will doubly increase the blessings over you.

"11Then all his brothers, all his sisters, and all those who had been his acquaintances before, came to him and ate food with him in his house; and they consoled him and comforted him for all the adversity that the LORD had brought upon him. Each one gave him a piece of silver and each a ring of gold." Job 42:11

Job was left alone; all his brothers and sisters left when he was going through the trials, through the worst storm; while he was sick, paralyzed, poor, and with no food, no one came around. However, after he passed the test, they all came back. There are many people like that today; those who abandon you when you are going through a trial. However, God allows it so that, in the midst of the desert, you learn to depend completely on Him.

ತ⇒ತ⇒ತ⇒

You will receive the same amount as you lost
during a test. You get it back multiplied.

ತ⇒ತ⇒ತ⇒

The devil stole from you, killed your family, left you on the street, and told you, "Now that you have lost it all, what will you do? How are you going to recover your money? How will you recover your family? Curse your God and die!" However, God tells you, "If you don't deny Me, if you don't leave Me, I will return everything to you multiplied."

෨෨෨

You only invest in people that endure the trial.

෨෨෨

Job's family returned to him and brought him offerings of money and gold rings. People will give you riches if you have overcome adversity because passing a test produces trust.

"12Now the LORD blessed the latter days of Job more than his beginning; for he had fourteen thousand sheep, six thousand camels, one thousand yoke of oxen, and one thousand female donkeys."
Job 42:12

Job's latter state, after the trial, was glorious and marvelous. This teaches that when you are going through difficult moments, you must not let bad thoughts get the better of you. The enemy will suggest ideas of suicide, or that you seek an escape in alcohol or drugs. He will say, "There is an easier way to solve your problems. Kill yourself. You will go on to a better life and your problems will end." However, the Bible says that whoever destroys his body, which is the temple of the Holy Spirit, will be destroyed by God. Therefore, the person that commits suicide is going against the will of the Creator. The act of giving and taking of life belongs to God alone. When we decide to commit suicide or to kill another person, we are transgressing and stomping on God's laws.

Suicide is a diabolical idea that seeks to destroy you and cut you off from God's life.

ॐॐॐ

Suicide is a permanent solution to a temporary problem.

ॐॐॐ

Times will get better. There are many more years and days to come after this problem. Remember what we said at the beginning. Every problem is temporary. It will not last forever. Make the decision to remain alive! Suicide is not the way out. Don't try to solve a temporary problem with a permanent decision. That is what Judas did. Jesus would have forgiven Him like He forgave Peter, and we would have received a Gospel according to Judas, but he took a definitive decision for a temporary problem and lost out on his future. How many people have you betrayed? How many have betrayed you and you are still alive? Today, there are people going through difficult moments and those thoughts come to mind, time and again. You must cast them out and take those thoughts captive to the obedience of Christ! There are still many blessings to come. There is still too much God wants to do with your life.

"¹³He also had seven sons and three daughters. ¹⁴And he called the name of the first Jemimah, the name of the second Keziah, and the name of the third Keren-Happuch." Job 42:13, 14

Remain faithful in the storm. Do not lose the blessing in the midst of your problems and even your children will be blessed.

Illustration: A family man began to experience financial troubles in his business and his wife divorced him because she did not want to sink into financial ruin with him. Five years later, she happened to see her ex-husband. It turned out that his company grew to seven times the size it was when she left him. Had she stayed with him, she would have been blessed and prospered, but she took a permanent exit to a temporary problem. The same thing happened to Job's wife. She cursed God and wound up dead. Had she remained with her husband, after the trial, she would have enjoyed the multiplied riches that he received. Job had beautiful sons and daughters and everything was multiplied.

"15In all the land were found no women so beautiful as the daughters of Job; and their father gave them an inheritance among their brothers. 16After this, Job lived one hundred and forty years and saw his children and grandchildren for four generations."
Job 42:15, 16

Endure the storm; persevere because there are seven times more blessings on the other side. After the storm, God gave Job an additional 140 years of life. Do not give up. Don't commit suicide. There are still many years ahead. You haven't seen anything yet. What Satan planned for evil, God will turn around for your good. Remember what the Word of God says, "All things work together for good for those that love God."

Testimony: Rodrigo graduated as an accountant but was then unemployed for six months. At a class of El Rey Jesus' Leadership Institute, the pastor prayed and decreed that all the unemployed would find a job within thirty days. After this, he received a call from an employment agency, because the lady that had previously interviewed Rodrigo told him that his face was continually coming to her mind, so she sent him out to a temporary job assignment. The job was only supposed to last a week but was then extended for two weeks, then an additional three, and finally for another twelve weeks. Later, after Rodrigo had been working for that same company for two years, a position became available for which he lacked the required experience. Nevertheless, his boss promoted him, even though there were other, better-qualified employees within the company.

In conclusion, it is obvious that our faith may be tested, but that said test is not a sign that we are in sin. Certainly, trials may come at some point in our life due to sin but, generally, the Bible teaches that these hardships are necessary. They come because we need to go through trials and difficulties for the glory of God and His nature to be manifested, His name be glorified, and so that He may entrust us with more glory, anointing, and authority. Remember that problems are temporary, not eternal, and that they happen to every Christian in the entire world. We must seek God, not for the fish and the bread, but rather because we love Him and want to see His Kingdom established. When we first came to Christ, we did so out of necessity. However, it is time for us to dedicate ourselves to seek, love, and serve Him for who He is.

We must understand that nothing can separate us from Him or from His love. There is a work, a purpose, a specific will of God for us, and it is imperative that we complete it. Many will leave, abandon, and betray us but we must continue. Success is measured by the ability to maintain a personal balance in times of crisis. We cannot become fearful. We cannot fall into insecurity and panic, for our heavenly Father protects and keeps us. In the midst of the storm, He is with us, testing our faith in order to entrust us with more riches.

Let us learn from Job who, though he was an upright man of integrity that feared the Lord and was unjustly attacked on every front, never cursed God, complained, or murmured. Job, therefore, passed the test and, as a result, God gave him seven times more than what he lost. He blessed him in everything and extended his life by many years so that Job might enjoy it all. That is what God has for each and every one of us. Lift up your head! Precious things are coming for you. The world is in crisis. There are moments of difficulty and everything is being shaken. The kingdom of darkness is trembling and the kingdom of man is falling apart. But if we are in the Kingdom of God, united to the will of the King, and serve Him despite our problems, past, or the injustices and betrayals suffered, we will remain firm and nothing will be able to defeat us. Christ in us, the hope of glory! In Him, we are more than conquerors!

CHAPTER VII

❧❧❧

Fed by Ravens

❧❧❧

When global economic crises come, people are quick to ask, "Why did this happen?" The people of God should have understanding about the times. They should be people that know what is going on, but more importantly, they should know how to deal with the moment with the guidance of the Holy Spirit. In this chapter, we will learn another way to receive the provision of God in times of economic hardship.

Why does crisis come?

Why do we have financial disasters? What can we do to overcome this? The world will experience different seasons, and we need to have prophetic eyes to recognize when we are entering a new one. We must learn to determine the causes that originate them and know where we are heading.

"¹Now the boy Samuel ministered to the LORD before Eli. And the word of the LORD was rare in those days; there was no widespread revelation." 1 Samuel 3:1

In the times during which Samuel grew up, the word of the Lord was scarce. There was no frequency of prophetic visions because there wasn't any prophetic guidance. There were no prophets to interpret the Lord, His motives, or His heart. There was no one who could express what He was doing and saying. When that happens, the people walk in darkness.

What does *vision* mean? Why was it rare?

Vision is the direct, fresh, and supernatural revelation of the knowledge of God. In other words, it is not just about teaching a doctrine or preaching another message. We are talking about a specific message for an equally specific moment. It is what God is saying and what is taking place in the spirit world at a determined time. In those days, there was no guidance because that fresh and direct revelation of the knowledge of God was missing. Today, the Holy Spirit wants to give us understanding so that we can know what God is presently doing and saying. This requires a prophetic revelation. A prophet is a person who feeds the Church through these means.

What has been the root of the financial disasters of the world?

Every reaction in the natural is the result of an action in the spiritual. If something happens in the spirit world, it immediately reverberates in the natural one. Let us take as an example the crisis of 2008 and 2009, where the economy of the United States entered a recession and strongly affected the rest of the world. It was God Himself who shook the financial system at the global level. I know this is difficult to understand, but I will explain it in detail. The crisis began in the United States because the American people were split in a mentality that ended up affecting the rest of the countries. From there comes the saying, "If America sneezes, the rest of the world catches a cold". The cause of this entire financial disaster was a battle in the spiritual world, between the Lord and *Mammon*, the spirit of greed.

What was this nation's problem?

The American people were divided at the religious, political, and economic level. Even as their principles were being broken, the main reason was money. God gave them the freedom to choose, and a large part of the people chose their wallets over moral goodness. Then the Lord decided to show whom the true God is, Him or *Mammon*–God or money. Therefore, He shook the stock market. It happened just like in the days of the prophet Elijah, when the Lord showed that He was the true God not *Baal*.

You might wonder, "But why didn't the men of God say any-thing so that we could save our money?" They did say something, but people did not pay attention to them. Many of them prophesied these things: "The financial system will crash. There will be a shaking in the banking system for a short period of time. There will be scarcity, and we will have a financial problem in the Nation, but it will be for a short time". It was not just one prophet that said it. Many did. When God speaks to us, He encourages us. He always warns us and gives us hope on one condition, that we correct our hearts.

And so, what is the fight about? *Mammon* **or Jehovah, Jezebel or Elijah**

"¹²And if you have not been faithful in what is another man's, who will give you what is your own? ¹³No servant can serve two masters; for either he will hate the one and love the other, or else he will be loyal to the one and despise the other. You cannot serve God and mammon." Luke 16:12, 13

Who can we not serve? Two masters. *Mammon* is a perso-
nified deity, a spirit of greed. Money in and of itself does
nothing, but the spirit that controls monetary movement,
Mammon, does operates against your life. *Mammon* takes a
human being and makes him or her the very personifica-
tion of greed. God gave us the freedom to choose between
Him and *Mammon*, i.e., Him or money. Somebody might
ask, "Was it the will of God?" No! It was not the will of
God. We know this because the prophets decreed otherwise; however, the people made their decision and God
cannot transgress their free will. Nevertheless, He can show
Himself as the true God.

How long can an economic shaking last? It might be a year,
six months, or two or three years. Remember that problems
do not last forever. In the meantime, what do we do? What
do we do while the unemployment rate keeps climbing?
What do we do while the government strips us of all financial aid? What do we do while we are going through a
crisis? Understand that you should not feel guilty if your
financial situation is not going well. Neither should you
say, "Perhaps I am in sin because I am tithing and offering
but I see no results." This is happening at a global level.
The most important thing is to know what to do.

Who is your Lord?

Jesus said, "*No one can serve two masters.*" The word *master*
means three things: owner, God, and absolute authority.
When we are in debt, the Lord is not our absolute God,
instead it is *Mammon* because he tells us when, how, and
what we can and cannot do. When you say, "Jehovah is my

Lord", you are establishing that, "God is my owner, my absolute Lord, my absolute authority, and I obey only Him."
So then, what do we do during tough times?

*"¹And Elijah the Tishbite, of the inhabitants of Gilead, said to
Ahab, 'As the LORD God of Israel lives, before whom I stand,
there shall not be dew nor rain these years, except at my word.'"*
1 Kings 17:1

Tishbe does not even appear in the map of Israel, which
means that it was not an important city. It was not even a
town, in fact, it was barely a village. *"...before whom I stand..."*
This is the prophet's ministry, to be in the presence of
God, to hear Him and declare His will and plans to the
people. *"...there shall not be dew nor rain these years, except at
my word."* How bold! If we apply this to modern times, who
would listen to what a stranger has to say? It is crucial to
understand the magnitude of this prophet's boldness. Why
did he go to tell the king that it would not rain? He did so
because if rain did not come to the land of Israel, famine
and drought would be imminent in the land. This stranger
stood before Ahab, king of Israel, and told him that it
would not rain unless it was at his word. Lord, give me that
authority! After this, Elijah went through three tests of
faith:

1. The test of *Cherith*

After he declared the word, God Himself told Elijah to
go into hiding while his prophecy was fulfilled, for he
had declared a very strong word. He, therefore, sent
him to *Cherith*.

How is our faith proven in *Cherith?*

The Hebrew word *Cherith* means a place of retreat. In other words, in times of drought it is best to retreat with God and seek His face. It is best to go on a *Cherith* with Him. In difficult moments, it is not time to play church. There is no time to lose. God told Elijah, "Separate yourself, go to *Cherith*. Go on a spiritual retreat. Consecrate yourself." How many of us workers and servants of God work and work but never have a *Cherith* with God? He tells us, "In the midst of hard-ship, it is time to retreat with me. It is time for you to bend your knees and worship Me. It is time for you to consecrate yourself. Leave everything and give me one day of the week. Give me two days of the week. Declare a fast and prayer and I will send you the ravens."

"*4...you shall drink from the brook, and I have commanded the ravens to feed you there. 5So he went and did according to the word of the LORD, for he went and stayed by the Brook Cherith, which flows into the Jordan. 6The ravens brought him bread and meat in the morning, and bread and meat in the evening; and he drank from the brook.*" 1 Kings 17:4-6

Here is the other key phrase: "*...I have commanded the ravens to feed you there.*" A raven is a black bird that eats the meat of dead animals. In other countries, they are also known as crows.

What does the Bible say about the raven?

"*41Who provides food for the raven, when its young ones cry to God, and wander about for lack of food?*" Job 38:41

Look at what Jesus said:

"24Consider the ravens, for they neither sow nor reap, which have neither storehouse nor barn; and God feeds them. Of how much more value are you than the birds?" Luke 12:24

God wanted to teach Elijah a lesson with the objective of preparing him to face *Baal*. Today, God wants to prepare us to confront *Mammon*. Jesus said, *"Consider the ravens..."* The word, *consider*, means to observe intently. The raven has no storehouse, does not know how to sow, and has no shovel to farm the land. Yet Jesus said, *"Of how much more value are you than the birds?"* So why are you worried? You are worried because *Mammon* has you by the neck with a system that denies God's power to give us provision and take care of us. You and I are worth more than a scavenging raven. If we trust in God, He will feed us and feed our children.

ॐॐॐ

God gave up everything because
of how immensely valuble we are to Him.

ॐॐॐ

"32He who did not spare His own Son, but delivered Him up for us all, how shall He not with Him also freely give us all things?" Romans 8:32

Therefore, *Mammon* cannot dictate our lives, make us lose sleep, or rob our peace. I trust in God, and just like he feeds the ravens every day, He will feed me and my children. He provides me with a roof over my head and brings me food as he brings me out of the crisis with good things. *"Do not fear little flock. Believe in the LORD your God, and you shall be established; believe His prophets, and you shall prosper."*

What is God's fresh revelation for this crisis?

God said: "Let Me prove who the real God is, *Mammon* or Me, the owner and Lord of your life. We will see who you trust in now." The Spirit of God will send ravens to tend to your needs. When you least expect it, God will send those scorned and "worthless" ravens to bless you. If you have trusted in God up to now, He will not let you be shamed. Fight the good fight! God already gave the order! Just wait! Do not dismay! Do not let your arms fall! Do not let your face reflect sadness! While you wait for the ravens to come, begin to give God the glory: raise your hands and bless Him for today is the day! God sends businessmen and businesswomen. The ravens are on the way. Single woman, the ravens are coming. Young person, the ravens are coming! You might not see them, but they are on the way. God will break *Mammon's* power over your life. Thank Him, because He has already sent the ravens to bring bread and meat to you in their beaks.

I want to make this declaration over the lives of those people who are reading this book and going through a crisis. As an apostle and prophet of God, I declare that unusual miracles will manifest in your finances. Contracts that were never awarded will now appear. Closed court cases begin to be reopened. Denied scholarships are being set loose now. You will receive a call tomorrow from the job where you were turned down because they now want to hire you. Father, thank You! The business you had lost is being restored, in the name of Jesus. The ravens come to your office. The ravens will come to your empty refrigerator. I declare it, I decree it, and establish that they come tomorrow!

2. The test of *Zarephath*

"⁷And it happened after a while that the brook dried up, because there had been no rain in the land." 1 Kings 17:7

The brook dried up because there had been no rain. Why did God do this? He did this because, many times, if God leaves you comfortable where you are, you will never go to the next level in His will. There are countless people in ministries that have already dried up. They are dry. It has been a while since it rained.

God spoke to many of you to start a business one or two years ago. You did so, and it went well. Sadly, the source of your success seems to be dry now and your business is no longer doing as well as before. You are now in financial distress, but you don't give up. You keep insisting. If the brook has dried up, you need to move on. Many are in a job that is going nowhere, and for a long time God has been saying, "I have more for you." Does this mean you should leave your current job? No, do not leave it until you have another one because God does not take you out of a place without giving you something better. Do not make that mistake.

Should you leave your job by faith? No, sir, that is not wise. There are many people, however, that God wants to take out of that dry brook.

"⁹Arise, go to Zarephath, which belongs to Sidon, and dwell there. See, I have commanded a widow there to provide for you." 1 Kings 17:9

He once again gives an order. First He commands the ravens and then a widow. Let us analyze this. We began with a raven that does not have to save up food or worry because God feeds it and now we see a widow. In Jesus' times, a widow was the poorest person in society. They were so poor that if they did not have any older sons to help them, they would be left homeless. God sends Elijah to a woman in such a condition for His next miracle. Look at what Jesus says about this.

"²⁵But I tell you truly, many widows were in Israel in the days of Elijah, when the heaven was shut up three years and six months..." Luke 4:25

What happened to Heaven? Have you ever experienced a time in which you felt like Heaven was closed to you?

"²⁵...and there was a great famine throughout all the land; ²⁶but to none of them was Elijah sent except to Zarephath, in the region of Sidon, to a woman who was a widow." Luke 4:25, 26

Why *Zarephath?* The word *Zarephath* in Hebrew is *Tsarephath,* and it means a refinery, a place of purifycation. It is a place where fire burns all impurity. Has it not happened to you that you leave from one place and go to another thinking it's going to get better only for things to get worse? What is God doing? God is saying, "Leave the brook at Cherith, which has dried up. Get up, obey, and go to Zarephath. In Cherith, you were with Me and retreated to seek My presence. In Zarephath, I will purify you." God sent Elijah to meet this specific widow, saying to him:

"9... I have commanded a widow there..." 1 Kings 17:9

Now let's take a look at the story of a poor widow:

"10So he arose and went to Zarephath. And when he came to the gate of the city, indeed a widow was there gathering sticks. And he called to her and said, 'Please bring me a little water in a cup, that I may drink.' 11And as she was going to get it, he called to her and said, 'Please bring me a morsel of bread in your hand.' 12So she said, 'As the LORD your God lives, I do not have bread, only a handful of flour in a bin, and a little oil in a jar; and see, I am gathering a couple of sticks that I may go in and prepare it for myself and my son, that we may eat it, and die.'" 1 Kings 17:10-12

What a sad story! This man was not sent to just any widow he found but to a specific one. When God connects you to people, do not look down on them just because they don't have money. They are the widows that will feed you, that will sustain you. Then God will raise them up as well and grant them a great provision. Just as God commanded the ravens, He will command a widow to sustain you. In the midst of crisis, you will go through the refinery, but while there, God will raise up a widow to provide for us; other times, He will use us as the widows to be the providers. This widow was waiting for him. When there is oil and a little bit of food, that is where God is waiting for you. That will be the person He uses to sustain you.

What is *Zarephath*?

Zarephath is the furnace of fire. It is difficult to have all types of luxuries one day only to wake up the next and see that not even one is left. It is hard to wake up knowing that yesterday your bank account was full but that now you can barely pay for the essentials, if that. Yet, in the midst of this, the message is that you cannot waver between two mentalities. Is *Mammon* your master, your god, and your authority, or is it Jehovah, your heavenly Father, the owner of silver and gold? Who will you trust?

God sent the ravens in the morning. They are flying in your house as you read this. God says, "You have sown, you have tithed and offered, and that raven is coming." He says, "Get out of there. If that ministry or business has dried up, get up and go to *Zarephath* where I want to purify your heart and your motives, where I want you to rise up with all power."

This is the word of the heart of God. Allow this to penetrate your spirit. In the midst of crisis, you are the sustenance for your family. Though they might not want you, though you might be persecuted and looked down upon, you are the one your family looks to and says, "What will you do during these difficult times?" Your heart should remain calm and trusting. If God has to raise rocks to feed you, He will do it. He *will* complete everything He promised to do. Trust in Him. Do not let fear creep into your heart. Do not worry about tomorrow. Sleep in peace and joy.

"¹³And Elijah said to her, 'Do not fear...'" 1 Kings 17:13

Here comes the condition:

"¹³...go and do as you have said, but make me a small cake from it first, and bring it to me; and afterward make some for yourself and your son." 1 Kings 17:13

Wait a minute! This man is crazy. What do you mean by telling the widow to give him first to eat the last bit she has before she dies? The prophet sought to test her faith. He had come out of *Cherith* in faith, and by faith in what God had told him, he asked this of the widow. I can take a step of faith, but if you don't take yours, we have a problem. Why did he ask the widow to give him the only thing she had left? He did so because if she ate her seed, she would die alongside her son. This is why you should never eat your last seed. Plant it wherever God tells you. Give it to Him.

"¹⁴For thus says the LORD God of Israel: 'The bin of flour shall not be used up, nor shall the jar of oil run dry, until the day the LORD sends rain on the earth.'" 1 Kings 17:14

What does this mean? *"...The bin of flour shall not be used up, nor shall the jar of oil run dry..."* In other words, Elijah told the widow: "If you obey in this, if you dare to sow what you have, you will reap for a long time". If you are in the middle of a crisis, sow. Sow a seed because no bank is safe. Nothing is safe. Everything can be shaken. Elijah was taking a leap of faith so that she too could jump. Perhaps it has happened to you that you have to pray for a person who needs a miracle even though you yourself have not received it. When this happens, the devil will often try to tell you, "But you hypocrite, you yourself need it..."and likewise you should reply, "This is a step of faith. We are all living by faith."

Testimony: A young man without a family, received a layoff letter from his job. On his last week of work, he said, "I am going to do what my pastor taught me." He gathered all the money he had left and sowed it. He took it to the altar at church. That week, he received a check for twenty thousand dollars. With this money, he started the business he now owns. He no longer works for someone else!

"15So she went away and did according to the word of Elijah..." 1 Kings 17:15

Note that the widow did not argue. She did not say, "You want to take my money, prophet? You are greedy, and you want to eat my food. Are you crazy?" She was obedient.

"¹⁵So she went away and did according to the word of Elijah and she and he and her household ate for many days. ¹⁶The bin of flour was not used up, nor did the jar of oil run dry, according to the word of the LORD which He spoke by Elijah."
1 Kings 17:15, 16

The word was fulfilled. What was the condition? It was for the woman to turn the last thing she had to eat into a seed and sow it in faith. We will do the same. Live in that sowing. God was not asking for a favor, rather He gave the widow an order. Sow your last seed!

3. The test of Carmel

Now for Elijah's third test, Mount Carmel. Remember this is a representation of what happens in the world with the economy and personal crisis.

What does *Carmel* mean? It means

Carmel means the garden of fruits.

"¹⁸And it came to pass after many days that the word of the LORD came to Elijah, in the third year, saying, 'Go, present yourself to Ahab, and I will send rain on the earth.'"
1 Kings 18:1

It had been three years since Elijah stood before the king and told him it was not going to rain.

Who was *Ahab*?

Ahab was the king of Israel; he was like a modern day

president, and would rule the whole nation. After three years and in the middle of a drought, God told Elijah, "You already went through *Cherith* and know what it was like to be fed by ravens. You were also in *Zarephath*, where you learned that I could even use a widow to feed you. Now there is no doubt. You know that I am your provider." Add up everything you have to pay in rent, food, insurances, the car, etcetera, and deduct it from the money you had. When you do this, you realize that God has provided, and it leaves no room for you to doubt that it was He who did it. God then sent Elijah to present himself before the king, because now He would send rain over the land. In the prophetic, rain always represents financial blessings as well as and the out-pouring of the Holy Spirit and God's power.

"2So Elijah went to present himself to Ahab; and there was a severe famine in Samaria." 1 Kings 18:2

Famine or scarcity in the natural is a prophetic reflection of what is going on in the hearts of the people who hunger for the Word of God. "They are not hungry for bread or food, but for My Word."

"3And Ahab had called Obadiah, who was in charge of his house. (Now Obadiah feared the LORD greatly. 4For so it was, while Jezebel massacred the prophets of the LORD, that Obadiah had taken one hundred prophets and hidden them, fifty to a cave, and had fed them with bread and water.)"
1 Kings 18:3, 4

Obadiah was a Jew who feared the Lord. He had not abandoned God for *Baal*, and he was in King Ahab's service. *Ahab* had a wife named *Jezebel*, and she was the one that truly controlled all of Israel. Moreover, because she was a pagan, she started widespread worship of *Baal*, the god of the elements, i.e., of the sun, the rain, and of fire. It was this woman who corrupted the hearts of half of the people, using her husband's throne to lead it to worship *Baal*. Israel would waver between the two powers, between Jehovah and *Baal*. One half of the people of Israel would say, "*Baal* is god". The other half would say, "Jehovah is God". Elijah then presented himself before *Ahab* by God's orders.

"*16*So Obadiah went to meet Ahab, and told him; and Ahab went to meet Elijah. *17*Then it happened, when Ahab saw Elijah, that Ahab said to him, 'Is that you, O troubler of Israel?' *18*And he answered, 'I have not troubled Israel, but you and your father's house have, in that you have forsaken the commandments of the LORD and have followed the Baals.'"
1 Kings 18:16-18

This is figurative of what we have today. Many people leave God and go to serve *Mammon*. It is time for the children of Jehovah to know who the true God is.

"*20*So Ahab sent for all the children of Israel, and gathered the prophets together on Mount Carmel." 1 Kings 18:20

Elijah, full of the Holy Spirit, decided to put an end to the people's division and lead their faith towards the one true God. Therefore, he proposed a challenge.

Presently, we are approaching a time when people no longer will believe tales. They want something feasible, something real. When someone with cancer or any other illness challenge you, you cannot say, "Allow me to fast and pray to see if it is the will of God". At that instant, you need to show who your God is. People are sick of religion. They want a real, visible, and tangible demonstration.

"²¹And Elijah came to all the people, and said, 'How long will you falter between two opinions? If the LORD is God, follow Him; but if Baal, follow him.' But the people answered him not a word. ²²Then Elijah said to the people, 'I alone am left a prophet of the LORD; but Baal's prophets are four hundred and fifty men. ²³Therefore let them give us two bulls; and let them choose one bull for themselves, cut it in pieces, and lay it on the wood, but put no fire under it; and I will prepare the other bull, and lay it on the wood, but put no fire under it. ²⁴Then you call on the name of your gods, and I will call on the name of the LORD; and the God who answers by fire, He is God.' So all the people answered and said, 'It is well spoken.'" 1 Kings 18:21-24

Why did Elijah present them with such a difficult challenge? They said that *Baal* was the god of fire and rain; nevertheless, it had not rained in three years and now they had to ask him to send down fire. God had been proving Himself, stopping the rain for approximately 42 months, and was now about to give *Baal* the final blow with the issue of fire. People today challenge us with their saints and beliefs and ask us for reasons to believe in our God. What do we do in that situation?

We are not going to wait for them to challenge us; rather, we will challenge the people. Let us go out there! Let us dare, like Elijah, to challenge *Baal's* followers and the ones who doubt. Ask the Lord to reveal to you the past of the people, a tough situation in their life, or something that no one else knows, and give them a word from God. The supernatural overcomes unbelief.

24Then you call on the name of your gods, and I will call on the name of the LORD; and the God who answers by fire, He is God.' So all the people answered and said, 'It is well spoken.'" 1 Kings 18:24

So the fight begins. This prophet was so bold! To do this, you need to know who your God is and who you are. *Baal's* worshippers said, "We serve the god of fire so this should be easy, so let us light him a few candles and he will answer quickly."

"26So they took the bull which was given them, and they prepared it, and called on the name of Baal from morning even till noon, saying, 'O Baal, hear us!' But there was no voice; no one answered. Then they leaped about the altar which they had made. 27And so it was, at noon, that Elijah mocked them and said, 'Cry aloud, for he is a god; either he is meditating, or he is busy, or he is on a journey, or perhaps he is sleeping and must be awakened.'" 1 Kings 18:26, 27

Illustration: When your santero neighbor takes a chicken and performs a sacrifice (he practices Santeria), tell him or her: "The blood of Jesus is more effective than the blood of that chicken." When your boss tells you,

"Your services are no longer needed. I am afraid we have to let you go," tell him, "God used you to feed me for a season, but now He will give me a better job". We need to know in who and where we are planted. Our God is strong and Almighty. Elijah not only gathered and challenged *Baal's* priests, but he also mocked them and their god. While they leaped about, cut themselves and bled, Elijah would laugh at them because their god did not answer. We can do the same. The gods of this century are impostors, just like the gods of those times. Only the Lord saves, heals, delivers, provides, feeds, restores broken relationships, and sup-plies all our needs. The God we serve does answer.

"29And when midday was past, they prophesied until the time of the offering of the evening sacrifice. But there was no voice; no one answered, no one paid attention." 1 Kings 18:29

The day will come when the people will cry out to their idols and no one will answer them. Days will come when people will surrender everything to their gods for an answer, for a miracle, but nothing will happen.

"30Then Elijah said to all the people, 'Come near to me.' So all the people came near to him. And he repaired the altar of the LORD that was broken down." 1 Kings 18:30

The key is in the altar. You can go to church, listen to the Word, and receive the fire of God, and God's presence that consumes, burns, destroys evil, and brings blessings will manifest. If, however, you live a godless life and leave your altar neglected all week, nothing will happen.

What did Elijah do to bring fire down from Heaven?

❖ **He fixed the ruined altar.**

You might say, "But I tithe, give my offerings, am a good person, and harm no one," but I ask you, "Is your altar repaired?" The altar was, and continues to be, the place where the tithes, offerings, prayers, intercession, and worship are brought. The altar we see in church is a physical one, where physical offerings are brought. In the spiritual world, however, there is an altar in the heart, where Jesus, the High Priest, receives our offerings and presents them to the Father.

The most severe sin of the people of God in these times is prayerlessness. It is crucial to fix and restore the personal altar. God always looks for an altar. What do Buddhists do when they open a restaurant? They put a big, fat *Buddha* for people to throw money at when they leave, believing this will bring them good luck. Where did they get that idea? They got it from God. As for you, do you have a place, an altar, where you can worship God in your house?

How is the altar broken?

When people degrade God's altar and introduce idols, it is ruined. The altar of God is holy. When you put other gods in your heart, in the same place where you worship God, you corrupt it, and God no longer descends there. If a person is living in sin, God will leave. Perhaps you have seen this in other people, but have seen no negative results, and ask, "Pastor, why didn't anything happen to them?" The answer is be-cause the altar is already ruined. When there is a holy man or woman of God, the person who does not enter the altar in holiness ends up dead.

"8'And when you offer the blind as a sacrifice, Is it not evil? And when you offer the lame and sick, is it not evil? Offer it then to your governor! Would he be pleased with you? Would he accept you favorably?' Says the LORD of hosts." Malachi 1:8

The people were giving God their leftovers God. Prior to the coming of Christ, people would present in sacrifice the lame, blind, and sick animals. When it was time for the offering, they would offer Him the animal with a limp, with a missing horn, or the blind one, and throw it on God's altar. The same happens today. People give God their leftovers, the change they received after paying for their groceries. They will spend an obscene amount of money when they go to the movies, buying drinks, popcorn, or chips, but think twice to give God what belongs to Him. To this God says, "My fire cannot come down under such conditions." There is one condition: we have to fix the altar, and give God the best, not the leftovers. Give Him the best of your time, your offerings, your worship, and your prayer. Every day, give God the best you have, and the fire will come down. God will bring a *suddenly*, but first you must fix your altar.

How is the altar fixed?

Give God the best, not your leftovers. Do not give Him the dirty, wrinkled up dollar bill. Give God what He deserves and how He deserves it. That way, He will intervene in your needs even while everyone else is in desperation. When you and your neighbor don't have a job, God will do a "suddenly" in your life and provide you the job you need. We have lost the virtue of honoring God. We are more fearful and respectful of a governor or a politician than of Jesus Himself. We see going to church the same as going to the movies. God, however, does not want the crumbs, the broken, or the old things that no longer work. He will not receive them! Give God the best of yourself. When you are going to praise Him, tell Him, "Lord, I bring praise to your altar and give you all I have, the very best of me." When you are going to intercede, say, "Lord, I am going to cry out in this altar. I will pour out my heart." When the time for sacrifice comes, the worshippers of Baal will cry out but no one will answer them. If you, however, have honored your altar, you will have an Almighty God whose hand will work in favor of your life. The blessings and rain will not come unless we repair the altar of God, beginning with our own altar.

What did Jesus say about the altar?

"²³Therefore if you bring your gift to the altar, and there remember that your brother has something against you, ²⁴leave your gift there before the altar, and go your way. First be reconciled to your brother, and then come and offer your gift." Matthew 5:23, 24

The altar is so holy that God will not receive our offering if we are in a fight with our brother.

What did Paul say about the altar?

"¹³Do you not know that those who minister the holy things eat of the things of the temple, and those who serve at the altar partake of the offerings of the altar?"
1 Corinthians 9:13

Those who work for God have the right to receive their provision from the altar. However, for there to be a balance, before putting someone there, God tests their heart. He does this to test if they serve for money or if they serve because they want to honor Him.

"¹⁴Even so the Lord has commanded that those who preach the gospel should live from the gospel."
1 Corinthians 9:14

"³¹And Elijah took twelve stones, according to the number of the tribes of the sons of Jacob, to whom the word of the LORD had come, saying, 'Israel shall be your name.'"
1 Kings 18:31

For God to descend with power, the altar must be prepared. The number 12 means order. God does not descend wherever there is disorder. What you are in the natural is what you are in the spiritual. If you are disorganized in the natural, you will also be disorganized in the spirit.

❖ Elijah prayed

"36And it came to pass, at the time of the offering of the evening sacrifice, that Elijah the prophet came near and said, 'LORD God of Abraham, Isaac, and Israel, let it be known this day that You are God in Israel and I am Your servant, and that I have done all these things at Your word.'" 1 Kings 18:36

Elijah did not make any of this up. He was obeying what God had ordered. In numerous occasions, we get ourselves in trouble because we do what we believe instead of what God orders. When He gives you an order, follow it regardless of how hard it might be. It is an order.

෨෨෨

He will fight for you
and bless the work of your hands.

෨෨෨

God answered with fire from Heaven

"37Hear me, O LORD, hear me, that this people may know that You are the LORD God, and that You have turned their hearts back to You again. 38Then the fire of the LORD fell

and consumed the burnt sacrifice, and the wood and the stones and the dust, and it licked up the water that was in the trench. [39]Now when all the people saw it, they fell on their faces; and they said, 'The LORD, He is God! The LORD, He is God!'" 1 Kings 18:37-39

This is what will happen in our neighborhood and in our nation when we demonstrate who God is. The people will say, "Jehovah is the true God." Their idols have a mouth but do not speak, they have ears but do not hear, but our God is alive. In the midst of famine and drought, our God will provide and fulfill His promise. Now is not time to murmur or complain, but it is time to bring down fire from Heaven; it is time to prove that our God is the real and genuine God. It is time to cry out and tell the world that Jehovah is Lord! Let the idols hear you, let hell hear you, let the demons hear you, let misery hear you, and let scarcity hear you. Jehovah is the Lord!

The first sign proving that *Baal* was an impostor was his inability to make fire come down, even though he was supposed to be the "god of fire". Elijah, however, had tremendous boldness and was full of the anointing of the Holy Spirit. He cried out to the Lord, and the fire consumed the sacrifice and the water over and around the altar. He, however, was not satisfied with that. He decreed rain to the king, even though *Baal* was supposed to be the god of rain. The rain represents blessings, revival, and financial provision. Elijah had gone through *Cherith*, then *Zarephath*, and now he was in *Carmel*. The prophet repairs the altar, causes fire to fall from heaven, and gathers then kills the prophets of *Baal*. Immediately after this, he hears that a great rain is coming. He then told the king to go eat and drink while he bowed down to birth out the rain.

"⁴¹Then Elijah said to Ahab, 'Go up, eat and drink; for there is the sound of abundance of rain.'" 1 Kings 18:41

What do I do in a time of crisis?

When crisis comes, you must run to have a *Cherith* with God, and wait for the ravens to feed you. After this, you must go through purification in *Zarephath*, where the widow will feed you. When the time of challenge comes, you, full of the Holy Spirit, are to prove that Jehovah is your God and not *Mammon*. Repair the altar, get on your knees, and seek God to birth out the rain of blessings.

Important advice in times of crisis:

* Do not get in debt. If you do not have the money to buy gifts for special parties, do not give a gift to anyone. God does not provide for the foolish.

* Work where you can. If you do not have a job and are offered one you do not like, take it anyway. Go and dig holes if you need to. The most important thing is to provide food for your children.

* Be a good steward of what you have. In times of crisis, we must pray for God to give us creative ideas to invest or make wise use of the money we have left.

- Do not stop sowing into the Kingdom of God. There are people who, when they go through economic crises, the first thing they do is hold back their tithes and offerings not knowing that they are cursing themselves and bringing more famine to their house.

- Go to *Cherith* and to *Zarephath*, where the ravens and the widow will feed you and God will glorify Himself.

- Live with an expectation. God's provision will come at any moment.

- Repair the altar. Give God your best and pray for Him to consume your sacrifice. After that, birth out in the Spirit the rain of provision from Heaven.

- Do not allow your heart to be divided between two thoughts. Is Jesus your Lord, your master, and absolute owner, or will you place your trust in *Mammon*? The widow could have chosen to eat the last bit of food she had and curled up to die; yet, she sowed in times of crisis. Our God is a God of order. He will not take away your children's milk and then fail to provide for them. Everything you sow in God is destined to bring you provision and multiplication. Once you have made the sacrifice, get in a birthing position and birth out the rain of blessings. Crisis is an opportunity to see the glory of God in our lives. It is an opportunity to expand our faith and see the manifestation of the power of God. Crisis is an opportunity to fix the altar, sacrifice the best we have, and see the fire of God fall and His rain come down.

CHAPTER VIII

ન્ઈ ન્ઈ ન્ઈ

Creative Ideas
to Prosper

ન્ઈ ન્ઈ ન્ઈ

I n times of crisis, we cannot continue to do the same things we do as in times of abundance. When we are confronted with a season of scarcity, we have to change our way of working and producing. One of the ways God has planned for this is through creative ideas. People who are faithful in bringing in their first fruits to the Lord and to honor Him with their money, have the right to expect to receive creative ideas from Him that will resolve their critical situation; this extends to the family, business, education, work, or any other area. For this to take place and for us to see this and not lose out on it, we must also go through a change in mentality and an uprooting of paradigms. We need to work in a different way because the times have changed.

The world has a paradigm regarding believers. It believes they are dumb people with no brains or aspirations. In fact, I myself used to think like that about Christians. Before I became one of them, I used to laugh at them, but that is no longer the case. God is raising a different generation. As I began to get involved and preach in the nations, I found the truth to be otherwise. In all the churches I have visited around the world, I have come upon several bright people in all areas of society. I found people in government, in business, and other people with brilliant minds. I have met Christian scientists, doctors philosophers, lawyers, writers, athletes, actors, and generals who were Christians. Others like them are presently receiving Jesus as their Lord and

Savior. I have seen Christian presidents, Christian senators, and great Christian businesspeople. Also, I have seen how many believers who were bound by a religiosity that did not allow them to pursue an education are now being set free from that manner of thinking and are preparing themselves. There was a time when some churches would preach that universities were from the devil because they taught people not to believe in Jesus. Similarly, they would argue that Jesus was coming soon and, therefore, that it was not worth it to waste their time in studying, etcetera. I have seen a large part of God's people come out of that mediocrity and seek to give Him the best. We Christians are an intelligent people!

The devil tries to place a barrier between us and the outside world and cause them to think and say, "Church is for the weak. The people that go to church are brainless, ignorant, and uneducated". Let me tell you that God is raising a new generation, one that will take dominion through creative ideas and implement them by means of the knowledge acquired through their education. Just like society itself, the Church is not just made up of illiterate people but also of all other types of people, from all levels of society.

What are creative ideas?

"[19]And my God shall supply all your need according to His riches in glory by Christ Jesus." Philippians 4:19

What does the phrase "riches in glory" mean? This expression does not refer to material things. It is not about divine provision by means of tangible things but about something greater. The term "riches in glory" is a Hebraic expression that means "creative ideas". God will supply us with every-thing we need by means of creative ideas. He is full of them, for it was with His ideas that He created the entire world and everything in it. Only our planet has an in-numerable amount of objects and creations, animate and inanimate, monumental and microscopic, visible and invi-sible, such as water, wind, and microorganisms. It all came from the creative ideas of God.

You might ask, "How will a creative idea pay my rent or for the house I am about to lose? What kind of business ven-ture should I start?" These are very valid questions, ones which we will answer throughout the reading of this book. First, know that in the Kingdom of God, everything begins with a seed. God will never give you a large business, one already finished and with all the work already done. It all begins with a seed. This seed goes to the ground, dies, ger-minates, blooms, and turns into a tree that later bears fruit in abundance. Every time it is pruned, it becomes stronger and more fructiferous. Likewise is the Kingdom. There are people who are waiting for God to take them out of a problem with a miracle that comes like by magic, but they should know that there is a big difference between magic and the supernatural power of God. Some people believe that He will suddenly send them a check to pay for their house. Of course, He can do it, and we will not limit Him, but there is still a great difference between magic and His supernatural power.

‡‡‡

A creative idea begins with a seed.

‡‡‡

What is magic?

Magic appears suddenly. For example, you need $1,000 and out of nowhere, you find ten hundred-dollar bills under your bed. God's supernatural aspect is something real, blessed, and everlasting. However, there are still believers who are so innocent that they think God will prosper them through magical acts, and are constantly looking at the ground, hoping to find money on the floor or believing God will put a piece of gold under their pillow. God will give us solutions to our financial problems through creative ideas. The Spirit of God is the only One that can perform a miracle per second and never repeat Himself because His creativity is endless. He Himself will give you the innovative visions to get out of debt, for your business to prosper, etcetera. In times of Crisis, we need God's creative ideas.

God gave mankind His creative power

"26Then God said, 'Let Us make man in Our image, according to Our likeness..." Genesis 1:26

God gave mankind authority over all things saying, "I have created you according to My image and My likeness." God did not make animals according to His image, but He did create mankind in His image and likeness, with emotions, a mind, feelings, and a will. We are greater than animals because we have an intellect. We have a creative, inventive capability. Animals act by instinct, while we act by reasoning, i.e., we have a mind. That makes us different. We have an intellect because God has an intellect. Ideas come from the mind of God. The Holy Spirit then deposits them in ours.

"27For as he thinks in his heart, so is he..." Proverbs 23:7

Another translation says: *"As a man thinks in his heart, so he is."* God says: "I made you in My image and likeness. You have a mind, and I will also give you the ability to create."

We are not talking about creating like God, but about the creative power He gave us to do new things that are yet to be developed in the natural world. God said, "If you are going to have dominion and lordship, to be fruitful and multiply, you will need a special quality. I will give you the power to create". Mankind can create in three different ways:

- **Through sexual activity**

  The man's semen and the woman's ovum unite to generate life—to procreate. As a result, babies are born and humanity multiplies.

- **Through words**

  "21Death and life are in the power of the tongue, and those who love it will eat its fruit." Proverbs 18:21

  The power of life and death is in our words, through which we can create a dark, negative environment or one full of glory, peace, joy, light, and much more.

- **Through God-given thoughts and ideas**

  Your thoughts produce a seed and your mouth produces the water that irrigates it and helps it grow. While you think, that seed grows, and as you talk, it begins to flourish.

Testimony: I preached a message based on this chapter to my church. Amongst the thousands that heard it, one in particular grabbed on to the word I gave about creative ideas. There was chaos at the airline where she worked, a problem they could not fix. However, God gave her an idea that was so good that they assigned her the task of training a whole section of the airline's personnel to work with that new idea.

What are the four stages to take dominion and lordship?

"28Then God blessed them, and God said to them, 'Be fruitful and multiply; fill the earth and subdue it; have dominion over the fish of the sea, over the birds of the air, and over every living thing that moves on the earth.'" Genesis 1:28

Here are described the four stages involved in taking dominion and lordship. This we do with the thoughts of God, by means of His creative ideas.

1. Be fruitful

The translation of the Hebrew word *parah* is: produce, bloom, increase, grow, and to be fertile. The words "**be fruitful**" literally mean to be productive. A fruitful person is productive. The word "**productive**" comes from two Latin roots: *pro*, which means for, or in favor of, and *duct*, which means channel. Thus, to be productive means to be a channel for, or in favor of, someone or something. He wants everyone to be channels He can use to bless others. We are to be instruments by which others can be blessed.

One day, Jesus wanted to eat of the fruit of a fig tree but it had none, so He cursed it and the fig tree dried up. The fruitless fig tree represents the religious external covering that people put on when they are not producing fruit for the Kingdom. There are people, who dress like sons and daughters of God, but in reality, their marriage is failing, their finances are in shambles, and their life is empty and disorganized. They go to church but they lack a relationship with the heavenly Father. All throughout the Bible, you see Jesus giving parables and illustrations about this type of people. His parables teach how we must be bearing fruit, multiplying and refusing to become stagnant. One example is the parable of the man who gave talents to his servants and left, only to come back later and have them each give account of what they produced. There are people who spend numerous years in the Gospel yet are grossly unproductive; their lives are unfruitful. In the Kingdom of God, rewards are given for three reasons.

- **For battles won.** When we read the book of Revelations, we find that all of God's rewards are given to those who overcome.

- **For faithfulness.** This is to constantly do the work that God has commanded us to do. If we have been faithful, every one of us will one day hear these words, "Good and faithful servant, enter the joy of your Lord." Faithfulness is a virtue for which we are rewarded in this life and the next.

- **For productivity within the Kingdom of God.** Paradoxically, if you say this to Christians today, they get offended. The fig tree gets offended when it is asked for fruit, but God created it to bear figs. What is the meaning of its existence if it is not functioning in what it was created for? At your job, you are paid to produce. If you do not fulfill the duties for which you were hired, you will be fired. Yet we go to church and become so religious that we say, "The pastor is asking me for too much". When the world pays us for the fruit we bear, how prosperous we can become! Then why do we become offended when God also asks us for productivity?

God created mankind and told them, "I want you to be fruitful and a channel of blessings to others." Essentially, His Word has always been, "I did not make you to grow fat and to seat on a church pew, complaining about everything that goes wrong or about how bad the situation is in the world". God did said, "You have My mind. I made you intelligent so that you can bear fruit and be productive". In every area of our lives, we need to be fruitful. Wherever we are, even in hard times, we need to be fruitful. Jesus said, "I want fruit."

We cannot be a blessing to others if we are fruitless. In order to be productive, you need to think outside the box, outside of the set pattern, outside of the *status quo*. Creative ideas come to bless others, to supply needs, solve problems, and improve the life of our neighbor. Most of us are financing someone else's ideas, but God is raising a generation that thinks outside the box—a pioneering people with new and creative ideas. That is what we call "new wine".

We will take dominion through our thoughts and creative ideas. In times of crisis or recession, do not do the same thing you have always done. Instead, begin to ask the Lord, "How can I do this now that I do not have a job? Spirit of God, please give me a creative idea to start a business." At times, God allows people to lose their jobs so they can take a leap of faith and launch their own business. If you are productive with a little, God will give you a lot more so you can multiply it as well. Ask the Holy Spirit to give you a creative idea, and He will be faithful to give it to you. He will even give you inventions and strategies! If you believe it, you will receive it.

"¹⁴For the kingdom of heaven is like a man traveling to a far country, who called his own servants and delivered his goods to them. ¹⁵And to one he gave five talents, to another two, and to another one, to each according to his own ability; and immediately he went on a journey." Matthew 25:14, 15

God has given us something with which to produce. Some of us received one, two, or five talents, according to our capabilities. Now what are we doing with that? Mostly, we are only paying for the ideas of third parties. One person came up with an idea, another person invented it, and now we are paying to be able to use their ideas. Well, it is time for God's people to ask Him for creative ideas so that others will pay us to use our ideas. Nevertheless, always keep in mind that it will not come all finished and gift-wrapped, ready to go out in to the market. The idea will come in seed-form, as an idea in your mind, something you have never seen before. That is when you will say, "Wow! I had never seen that before! I had not realized that! I am going to do it!"

2. Multiply

Multiply is the second step in taking dominion through creative ideas. The word *multiply* is the translation of the Hebrew word *rabah*. It has many meanings include-ing abundance, growth, gain, increase in any aspect, as well as to dominate, enlarge, surpass, become greater, and become numerous.

❧❧❧

You cannot multiply what you
have not borne fruit in or produced.

❧❧❧

God gave you an idea, and it came to your heart but you have done nothing about it. If God gave you an idea, write it down, put it in to practice, obey God, and you will begin to bear fruit. When we receive an idea to bear fruit, then multiplication will come, that is, we will multiply our production.

Illustration: On a certain occasion, a man was in his garage mixing syrups and sweet drinks. When he tasted it, he really enjoyed the flavor and gave some to his wife and neighbors, and it turned out that everyone really liked it, too. That was how *Coca-Cola* was born, and it is now a multi-million-dollar company.

Many people might say, "Pastor, that took a long time, and I need to solve this problem right now!" Big blessings start with a small seed, with a creative idea that becomes fruitful, and then starts to multiply. Remember that during the time of a drought, Elijah was fed by the ravens. Then, when the rain finally came, it all started with a small cloud the size of a clenched fist.

Illustration: A young man was just watching the landscape though one of the windows of his house, when he came up with a creative idea. He developed it, it bore fruit, and then he shared it with others and multiplied it. Now, all throughout the world, people pay to use the *Microsoft Windows* system, created by *Bill Gates*. Currently, he is one of the richest men in the world, and has dominion over presidents and entire nations. All of this came thanks to a creative idea and the desire to produce. Lord, give me a creative idea! It is time for others to pay me! Did you know that *Elvis Presley* produces more money now that he's dead then when he was alive because of his music sales? A single idea from God is enough to transform your future, and the Holy Spirit is loosening those ideas over His children. Receive them!

3. Fill the Earth

This is the same creative idea that Jesus gave us to preach the Gospel of the Kingdom.

"⁸But you shall receive power when the Holy Spirit has come upon you; and you shall be witnesses to Me in Jerusalem, and in all Judea and Samaria, and to the end of the earth."
Acts 1:8

We need to fill the world with the Gospel of the Kingdom of God. If *Coca-Cola* has done it, why can't the glory of Jesus, which is the answer to every problem, do it, too? Likewise, if God has given you a creative idea in a specific area, and it has been successful, it is time to make it fruitful. Once it becomes fruitful, it is time to multiply its production. God's desire is to fill the entire Earth with that invention, creative idea, or product. In the same manner, we must fill the Earth with the Gospel of the Kingdom.

Illustration: King Jesus International Ministry began as a creative idea from God with a church in Miami. Once we received this idea and put it in practice, we became fruitful and began to be a blessing to others. Thereafter, the Lord sent us out to multiply in the area that we were bearing fruit in. The local church began to grow in great numbers, and we started to send out our spiritual children to open both daughter and satellite churches throughout the United States. We also began to take churches under our spiritual covering that reproduce the same pattern as our church does, all throughout the world. Nowadays, we have multiplied ourselves in 24 countries, and we continue to fill the Earth with the vision or creative idea that God gave us to establish His Kingdom here.

4. Subdue the Earth

The word, *subdue,* means to force into submission and to exercise dominion and lordship. *Microsoft's* owner, *Bill Gates,* has dominion over the entire world. He and his company constantly receive millions and millions of dollars. The last time a study was made, he was earning around $40,000 per minute. It all began with the idea of a window. His work multiplied so much that now he no longer needs to do anything. His company has a sustained growth that multiplies itself. So what are we waiting for, we the believers who have an Almighty and creative God? What are we waiting for? We need to start taking dominion and lordship by means of multiplication of creative ideas, concepts, and thoughts given by God. Satan fights so that individuals would look at their generation differently than God does, because if the devil can control their way of thinking, he can control their lives. The devil does not want you or me to use our minds, especially not the mind of Christ. Look at what Jesus said:

"8So the master commended the unjust steward because he had dealt shrewdly. For the sons of this world are more shrewd in their generation than the sons of light." Luke 16:8

When I read this for the first time, I got upset. I said, "Wait a minute! How can unbelievers be shrewder than us?" Well, Jesus said it! I asked Him, "Lord, how so?"

His reply was, "Yes, they are more shrewd...in their own territory". In other words, if you take worldly ideas and try to apply them to the Church, they will not work. However, God also told me, "If you take My ideas and apply them in their territory, you will be more shrewd than they!" Thus, that is the reason why God wants to loosen those concepts and ideas. We need to be wise in the use of Kingdom principles and creative ideas from God. That is our territory! That is our Kingdom!

Marxist communist ideas, as well as Darwin's evolutionary ideas, govern a large part of our world, controlling nations and influencing universities. Satan took those ideas and spread them world-wide in order to gain control of the people. Communism does not work because the only effective government is the Kingdom of God. Evolution has never even been proven, nor will it ever be. We do not come from a monkey, we come from God. New Age says, "The power to create is within us." Lies! It is not in us; rather, God has that power and He gives it to us in the shape of creative ideas to materialize the things He already created in the heavens. It is not through our mind that we create, but through the thoughts that the Holy Spirit puts in us. It is for that reason that the Bible says that we are administrators of His riches. It is though those riches that we will subdue the Earth, and put all its resources and benefits to work towards the Kingdom of God.

If you have never opened a business, why don't you say, "Lord, during these times of crisis, please give me a creative idea, something unusual, that others will pay me to have"? In the midst of this, the world needs to know that the God we serve is creative, that He is a brilliant God. We are not descendants of monkeys, we were made in the image of God and He wants to loosen creative ideas in our minds. He wants us to be productive for us to be a channel of blessings to others. Do not be sterile. Be fertile in everything you do. Let everything you touch reproduce, and later, multiply. Take dominion! Take lordship! Take control over Creation!

Satan's plan is to convince believers they are worthless. If he can diminish people's self-esteem and make them think they are dumb and worthless, he can continue to ruin this world. Satan is already defeated, but he does not just give up. He wants to take our inheritance, making us believe that we have no value. His lies have subdued many of the children of God. Open your eyes! God has given you creative ideas to take dominion and lordship. The enemy wants to raise a stronghold in your mind so that nothing creative can come out of you. God, however, says, "If you are going to take dominion, you need to first understand your worth". The devil whispers lies to you all the time, and you believe them, saying, "This is too hard. That idea is not from God. That is my flesh. That can only be done by great businesspeople who know how to manage a company but I am uneducated and don't even know where to start. I will lose the little bit of money I have left". Satan will try to erase the worth of your existence from your mind. He will try to twist what you think of yourself. He wants to stop you from thinking like a son or daughter created in the Father's image and likeness. He does not want you to discover that you are worth so much that Jesus came to die on the Cross for you. He wants to prevent you from reconciling with the Father, and He specially does not want you to take back the dominion God gave Adam in the Garden of Eden.

Illustration: If I take a $100 bill and kick it, step on it, wrinkle it and dirty it, does it lose its worth? Surely you have gone through difficult times. You have been persecuted, you have faced hell itself, you have been broken, tired, wrinkled and wounded, but I ask you, "Have you lost your worth?" The value of the $100 bill remains intact and yours does, too. You continue to be God's child, a co-heir with Christ, seated in heavenly places to reign. The bill's worth continues to be $100, and you continue to be an heir of the King of kings. Through His blood, Christ made you a new creature. Rise and shine because your light has come! The Holy Spirit of God speaks to you. Your value has not changed because Jesus paid for you with His own blood.

God's creative ideas cannot flow in a heart that thinks it is worthless or one that is insecure because of problems and the things that are happening in the world. I know that many of you identify with this because you are going through hard times, but understand that the $100 bill remains the same. You can go to a store with it and make your purchase. You can go to a super-market and use it as if it had just come out of the bank. Likewise, you have a purpose in life. You are not here by coincidence. Your worth has not changed. While the devil succeeds in making you think you are worthless, you will be thrown on the floor and stepped on. However, if you think like God thinks, if you have the mind of Jesus Christ, you will rise from bankruptcy by the same power that Jesus Christ was raised from the dead. You will rise with the power to overcome death in your business, in your relationships, and in your projects.

There is life in Jesus, and everything He touches resurrects. God is raising a different generation, people who understand the times, who know when to invest, when to buy, and when to sell.

When God created the world, He spoke to the substance or material with which He would make it and to the environment where it would dwell and receive its sustenance. That is, when He created the fish, He spoke to the sea, because that would be its habitat and from there would come its nourishment. When He created the trees, He spoke to the ground, and if you take a tree out of the ground, it dies because that is where its nourishment comes from, as it feeds from the Earth. When He made the stars, He spoke to the firmament, etcetera. However, when He created mankind, he did not speak to the firmament. He did not speak to the waters nor did He did not speak to the heavens or to the Earth; rather, He spoke to Himself.

He is the substance of our creation, and our spirit is in Him. God is the source that nourishes and edifies us. He said, "*Let Us make man in Our image and likeness.*" He continued by saying, "He will not be like the animals; rather, he will have a mind, will, and emotions. He will govern Creation and step on Satan's head. I will give you the creative ideas to subdue the Earth, to be fruitful, and to fill all the territories I have given you."

Stop thinking you are worth little or nothing. Think differently, act differently, and get out of Satan's box. Impress the world! Tell them who your God is. The world is looking at the fruit. How is it possible for us to call ourselves believers and, in the midst of a crisis, be as nerve-wrecked and as desperate as the ones with no God? There are times of emergency where people have nothing to eat and that is what the Church is there for, to help them. Our ministry has a budget designed for this. However, at this time, I am giving you the tools you need to never live off of another person's charity again, nor by ravens or widows. The world wants solutions. Everything is being shaken. It is time to seek God! It is time to rise up and recognize our worth! It is time to serve our society with creative ideas, ones that produce new jobs, raise the economy of the nation, and bring a structural reformation to this century! We the children of God are worth a lot because we were bought at the price of His blood! I invite you to pray to God and ask the Holy Spirit to give you creative ideas for your personal life, your family, your business, and your ministry. Write them down and take a step of faith, obeying those ideas and carrying them out.

In summary, we can say that:

* God is raising a generation of educated, intelligent, and capable believers who will take dominion of the Earth by means of creative ideas.

- Creative ideas are the riches of glory in Christ Jesus. If we are in Him, His ideas come to our mind and we are able to do great things.

- God blesses His people by means of creative ideas. These must be put in practice and developed. We must then bear fruit in them and multiply them to bless others.

- Thanks to the power given by God, mankind can create through sexual activity, words, and through the ideas that He puts in to the minds of people.

- The four stages for mankind to take dominion and lordship over Creation are: be fruitful, multiply, fill the Earth, and subdue it.

- In the Kingdom of God, rewards are given for battles won, faithfulness, and for productivity.

- To develop God's creative ideas, you must know your value as a son or daughter of God and then take dominion over Creation by means of the creative ideas He puts in your mind.

- In the midst of a crisis, a Christian should not panic, but rather go to the presence of God so that He can give him creative ideas to come through victoriously.

CHAPTER IX

☙☙☙

The Helmet

of Hope

☙☙☙

I n January of 2009, a suicide shook one of Germany's most influential families. One bad blow in the stock market and the fear of shame before his peers drove Adolf Merckle, ranked by *Forbes* as number 96 in the list of the world's richest men, to end his life by throwing himself in front of a train. This is today's world; a world of crisis and instability, full of fear, anxiety, and uncertainty. No one feels secure in regards to the future. Everyone is afraid of what is to come. This anxiety and fear have touched even our very doors and have entered the homes of many of the children of God, though the Word says that no plague would touch our dwelling. Therefore, in this chapter, we will learn how to protect our mind from bad news and how to believe and manifest the promises of God.

The apostle Paul spoke to the church of the Ephesians, teaching them to use the armor of the Spirit. He did this by making a reference to the roman soldiers' attire of that time. It bears mentioning that, as stated in the first verses, it is not God who puts the armor on us, but *we ourselves* who don it.

"10Finally, my brethren, be strong in the Lord and in the power of His might. 11Put on the whole armor of God, that you may be able to stand against the wiles of the devil. 12For we do not wrestle against flesh and blood, but against principalities, against powers, against the rulers of the darkness of this age, against spiritual hosts of wickedness in the heavenly places. 13Therefore take up the whole

armor of God, that you may be able to withstand in the evil day, and having done all, to stand. [14]Stand therefore, having girded your waist with truth, having put on the breastplate of righteousness, [15]and having shod your feet with the preparation of the gospel of peace; [16]above all, taking the shield of faith with which you will be able to quench all the fiery darts of the wicked one. [17]And take the helmet of salvation, and the sword of the Spirit, which is the word of God." Ephesians 6:10-17

Thus, our armor has six components. Note that it does not mention any pieces to cover the back, only the parts that cover the waist and the top of the legs. This reveals two things to us.

- We are supposed to confront our enemy face to face.

- The only time when we are vulnerable is when we give our backs to the enemy. In other words, if you put on the armor daily, but turn around, your whole back is vulnerable, and the enemy will have the opportunity to hurt you.

This chapter deals with only one piece of the armor, which is known as the Helmet of Salvation.

What is a helmet?

The roman armor's helmet was a tough headgear lined with sheets of metal and was used to protect the head and parts of the neck. You can go to war and have the sword and the shield, have your feet covered by sandals, and your chest covered by the breastplate, but if your head is unprotected, your enemy can strike you there one time and defeat you.

Why is it necessary to protect our head?

Verse 12 says we do not wrestle with flesh and blood but with spiritual hosts of wickedness. The head represents the mind. It is the place where thoughts and emotions are generated. The mind is the battlefield. If you are going to fight without putting on the helmet, your mind will be vulnerable. It does not matter how sharp your sword is. The darts the enemy sends to people's minds are strong enough to discourage a person in just a few moments.

Illustration: You are worshipping God when, suddenly, a dirty thought enters your mind. Then you say, "I do not want to think about that", but the dart did its damage, for it destroyed your inspiration to worship God.

What is humanity's problem during a crisis?

People's biggest problem in the midst of a crisis is their mind. The enemy attacks there so that it would seem like there is no way out, so that people think they have reached the end. This is what happened to that German billionaire. He could not cope with the mental pressure of what was happening. Satan sent him one dart after another until he took a permanent action for a temporary problem. He became depressed and committed suicide.

"8...putting on the breastplate of faith and love, and as a helmet the hope of salvation." 1 Thessalonians 5:8

As stated, the helmet of salvation is also referred to as the helmet of hope of salvation.

"¹³And now abide faith, hope, love, these three; but the greatest of these is love." 1 Corinthians 13:13

What is hope?

Hope is a precise mental expectation of something good. God has provided a protection for our mind, the helmet of hope. You might say, "But I am already saved." However, the helmet of the hope of salvation is not automatic; rather, we need to put it on. The evidence is in that the thoughts in your mind have you in fear, in affliction, and in sickness; but, when you activate the helmet, peace comes to your mind and allows you to see Jehovah's salvation.

Where are love, faith, and hope located?

Faith and love are found in the heart. You cannot love or believe from your mind. Hope, however, is located in the mind. In light of this, there are many people who believe they have faith, but all they have is a mental belief. I often have people come up to me and say, "Pastor, pray for me because I am sick." I ask them, "Do you have faith?" they reply, "Yes, I have faith". However, if they did, they would already be healed. What that person has is mental faith, and that does not work; only hope works.

How does faith travel from the mind to the heart?

Look at the results in your life. How many times have you believed and prayed for something but failed to receive what you expected? If you need to prove to somebody that you have faith, you still lack it. Faith comes through confession, i.e., from speaking what you believe. This is the Hebrew learning system. For a person to learn and have their faith travel from the mind to the heart, they have to repeat what they believe two or three times. When you are able to say it without struggling, it is because it has made its way to your heart.

Remember that faith comes by hearing the Word of God. What you speak and repeat all the time is what enters your heart. Unbelief also comes from hearing. What do people say in times of crisis? "...this is terrible; we cannot go on like this. I do not know what will happen. This crisis will ruin us." If you are constantly listening to this, it will travel from your mind to your heart and turn into that kind of faith. All of a sudden, you will say effortlessly, "This is terrible. We cannot go on like this. I do not know what will happen." What is the problem? If the mind is not delivered, but rather is full of thoughts of depression, low self-esteem, and of anxiety, the person will speak accordingly and that will make its way in to their heart.

"¹⁰For with the heart one believes unto righteousness, and with the mouth confession is made unto salvation." Romans 10:10

Therefore, faith and love are in the heart but hope is only in the mind. Nevertheless, by the confession of our mouth, hope travels from the head to the heart, where it activates our faith. Hope not founded in faith in Jesus is deceitful.

"²⁷...Christ in you, the hope of glory." Colossians 1:27

Thus, when you open your mouth, what you are doing is bringing that mental hope to your heart. We do this by confessing.

"[11]For I know the thoughts that I think toward you, says the LORD, thoughts of peace and not of evil, to give you a future and a hope." Jeremiah 29:11

The Lord says, "My plans are of peace, of life, and to give you a future and a hope." Hope is in the mind, and that is why the apostle Paul tells us that we must protect it with the helmet of salvation.

Where or in whom is our hope?

Before we came to Jesus, our condition was godless, faithless, and hopeless. We had a reason to be pessimistic, but, now that we are in Christ, by nature we must be optimistic.

"[12]...you were without Christ, being aliens from the commonwealth of Israel and strangers from the covenants of promise, having no hope and without God in the world." Ephesians 2:12

Before Jesus entered our hearts, we lived in the world and were far off from His covenants.

"[13]But now in Christ Jesus you who once were far off have been brought near by the blood of Christ." Ephesians 2:13

Illustration: On a certain occasion, a woman asked me to pray for her. While she explained her need to me, the Lord showed me that she spoke like a person from the world. She expressed herself as a person with no faith, no Christ, and no hope. When we are hopeless, we behave like worldly people and deny Jesus. Our confession becomes, "The doctor says I am sick. I am also about to lose my job. I am going through tough times. There is no end in sight. This is horrible! I am doing badly. I am losing my house." Paul, however, says: *"Christ in you, the hope of glory."*

Many place their hope on a president, on their job, or on their boss; but, the Word says something different. It does not matter how much the world is shaken. It does not matter how grim it gets or how bad the economy is. Rather, it is about Christ in us, the hope of glory! Do not behave like an unbeliever. You are a son or a daughter of God!

ॐॐॐ

The Christian with no hope
denies Jesus Chris and is
worse than an unbeliever.

ॐॐॐ

There are two types of people in the world: pessimists and optimists. I grew up being pessimistic. I was raised that way. Moreover, I was trained to be pessimistic. In my house, being optimistic was a "sin". When I told my dad that I wanted to study, he replied, "With what money? Who do you think you are? Are you crazy?"

Illustration: Two individuals see the same glass of water. The pessimist says, "It is half-empty." The optimist says, "It is half-full."

There is no place for pessimism or depression. If you have lost everything, will you curl up and die? Will you surrender to depression? Or will you shout out to Heaven, "Christ in me, the hope of glory!" Say this out loud, "The God who was with me yesterday is with me today." It is not time to put hope on man but on Jesus. He is our hope of glory. There are people who complain and say, "Pastor, but the economy is bad! Everything is bad". I tell them to be quiet and to start being optimistic. They say, "Pastor, it's so cloudy." Then my reply is, "Good! It's about to rain!" People say, "My finances are in bad shape." We, however, should shout, "This is the day where God will manifest His power."

What type of thoughts does God have? God has thoughts of peace and hope to give us a successful future. You must be optimistic. Put on the helmet of hope and declare, "My future is glorious. A thousand will fall to my right and ten thousand to my left, but it shall not reach me. He who dwells in the secret place of the Most High shall abide under the shadow of the Almighty. I am going to enter this season with a mental expectancy of something good." The thoughts of God are of peace. The thoughts of God are of prosperity and blessings. There is hope! Confess it with your mouth so that it reaches your heart. Why are we still thinking in a pessimistic manner? We do so because we were taught to think that way and because the enemy has our minds bound with fear, hopelessness, depression, anxiety, and confusion.

"¹When the LORD brought back the captivity of Zion, we were like those who dream." Psalms 126:1

Prisoners have a hard time dreaming and hoping. Until your mind is free, you will not have hope. You need to be delivered and then retrain your mind to be optimistic. It is not automatic. Your mind is corrupted with fear, trained to constantly think about misery.

What is the Biblical foundation for having a living hope?

"28...we know that all things work together for good to those who love God, to those who are the called according to His purpose." *Romans 8:28*

There are two conditions needed for this promise to be yours and to be fulfilled. God never makes promises without conditions.

- Love God.
- Be aligned with His purpose. God's chief purpose is to establish His will on Earth.

If you meet these conditions, everything bad that happens to you will be used by God and turned into good. This is a verse that promises us hope. Take the sword, put on the armor, and fasten the helmet of salvation. Why the helmet? We put on the helmet because, when the enemy sends darts your way that say, "You are not coming out of this one. It is too hard. No one in your family has been able to do it. You will end up dead or in prison..." you must be protected. Otherwise, you will not have a clear mind to use the sword. You might have the sword out of its sheath and say, "I bind you, devil. I cast you out." However, that is not enough. You must also put on your helmet.

How do we put on the helmet of hope?

It is very simple. You just need to say, in your own words, a prayer like this, "Lord, in the name of Jesus, I put on the helmet of hope, and I believe that my future is glorious, because Your plans for me are of blessings, health, and of peace. Father, I thank You because this year will be better than the last. I know that the plans You have for me are great. In the name of Jesus, I declare that all things will work together for good. Even if I lost money, it will still work out for good, because I love You, I love Your people, and I want to establish Your Kingdom on Earth."

What is the first thing we must do?

Before everything else, we must ask God for forgiveness for our negative confessions. Remaining sick or healthy is the product of our mouth. Faith comes by hearing the Word of God. Get up in the morning, knowing that hope is precisely the mental expectation of something good. When you go to work, declare, "Something good is coming for me today. I speak to my body and declare that I am the head and not the tail. I am above and not beneath. The blessings will reach me, overtake me, and overflow my cup. Everything will work together for my good because I love the Lord."

"12 Rejoicing in hope, patient in tribulation, continuing steadfastly in prayer." Romans 12:12

Look at the role hope plays. If you do not have hope, it is as though you were an unbeliever, like any other idolater. That is, you have to rejoice and look towards the future with joy for what is to come. This is a mental attitude, because hope is in the mind. This is the helmet.

"¹³Now may the God of hope fill you with all joy and peace in believing, that you may abound in hope by the power of the Holy Spirit." Romans 15:13

What are the signs of hope?

"¹⁷Thus God, determining to show more abundantly to the heirs of promise the immutability of His counsel, confirmed it by an oath, ¹⁸that by two immutable things, in which it is impossible for God to lie, we might have strong consolation, who have fled for refuge to lay hold of the hope set before us." Hebrews 6:17, 18

In these two verses, God mentions two unchanging things.

- His Word
- His oath

God did not just speak it; rather, He also confirmed it with an oath. These verses have two key points.

- **Hope is a grip.**

  What is a grip? A grip is something one holds on to. Thus, it is not just about using hope to protect our mind from the daily bombardment of bad news and pessimistic predictions, but also to grab a hold of what God is saying to His people.

  "⁵⁰Now Adonijah was afraid of Solomon; so he arose, and went and took hold of the horns of the altar."1 Kings 1:50

Hope is a place of refuge. In the Old Testament, the horns of the altar were the place that men would flee to and grab a hold of when they were being pursued by their enemies. If they were able to grab on to them, they could not be touched. The horns were in the altar, inside the Tabernacle.

From the previous verse, we learn that Solomon was chasing Adonijah because he was a traitor; yet, he grabbed the horns of the altar. Salomon sent for him and commanded his troops to wrench him from the horns and forgave him. This is what happens when you are at the feet of Jesus, in the altar with Him. The gates of hell are unable to touch you.

What are the horns of today?

Our altar is found where God's presence can be felt, and the horns are our hope in Christ. At that time, a man being chased by his enemies would find no safer place than the horns of the altar. Keep in mind that it is not just any part of the temple, or of the altar, but rather only the horns. If we apply it to daily life, hope is a place of refuge.

While there is a world that commits suicide because of going bankrupt, is depressed by bad news or due to a seemingly meaningless life, that is bound to drugs or lost in its sin, we have a Christ as our hope of glory. These are the horns of the altar of God. Jesus said: "Nothing can separate them from My hand." If you hold on to Him, that will be your hope. Come rain, hail, or snow, though Earth or hell tremble; if the world falls over or an atom bomb explodes, you can be sure that He is your best refuge in the world. Though the devil screams, cries out, or roars, Christ in us is the hope of glory. When we grab a hold of Him, we have nothing to fear.

The Bible teaches that not finding anything or anyone greater by which to swear, God swore by Himself. If you take hold of this promise, Heaven and Earth will pass but what He promised will be fulfilled. When hell itself comes against you, when you are pressured on all sides and don't know where to go, run to the altar and grab a hold of the horns! Christ is your hope.

◆ Hope is an exceedingly strong counsel

"¹⁹This hope we have as an anchor of the soul, both sure and steadfast, and which enters the Presence behind the veil."
Hebrews 6:19

Hope is an anchor for the soul. Hope in what? Hope in Jesus. Why do boats need an anchor? They need one because, if they are not held to something firm, the waves of the sea will pull them to its depths. There is nothing in a ship that can keep it stable against the waves except an anchor. It penetrates the waves and latches on to something solid.

"²⁹...fearing lest we should run aground on the rocks, they dropped four anchors from the stern and prayed for day to come." Acts 27:29

An anchor ends in two sharp points, which are used to sink it in the sand, or to have it attach to something, and thus keep the boat in place. A boat without a firm hold will be pulled by the tide because nothing will support it. Hope is an anchor that penetrates the waters until it finds something solid to grab on to. The water represents an insecure, unstable world, full of anxieties, doubt, and worries—a world without hope. This anchor is hope, which is cast and it latches on to the rock. The rock is symbolic of Christ; as a result, our hope is in Him, the Cornerstone. When things are not going well, when relationships begin to be shaken and your ship is being tossed by the sea, cast the anchor of hope and grab a hold of the Rock.

There are problems and difficult circumstances out there. People are nervous and depressed. There is uncertainty, anxiety, and worries. Those who have money hold on to it at all costs. Those who don't have any money seek out the witch, the soothsayer, or the seer. They run anywhere in search of salvation, but their ship remains unstable and looks like it will sink.

ৡৡৡ

*God's advice for these times is
to anchor ourselves to Jesus, the strong Rock.*

ৡৡৡ

What is the soul composed of?

The soul is the seat of the emotions, will, and the mind. When your emotions tell you, "Things are not well.

This is getting difficult", grab on to the Rock, for though giant waves may come, you will not perish.

There is nothing in this world that can give us stability unless it is the anchor of hope in Jesus Christ. Pick it up, cast it in the waters, and grab on to the unshakeable Rock of the ages! The amount of money you possess will not make the difference, nor will the types of insurance you have, the number of alarms you activate, or the security you hire. Without hope, you will be floating aimlessly. If you lost your job, cast the anchor. If you lost something in your life, cast the anchor. Grab on to the Rock. The water represents the times, which are constantly changing. The rock represents eternity, which never changes. When you are in Christ, you have a right to fasten your anchor, your hope, to Him, and no storm will be able to move you. Without hope, there is no place of refuge. Without hope, there is no Christ in you. Without hope, there is no salvation. We need to train our mind to think, "Christ in me, the hope of glory." Can you see yourself better in the future? Can you see the changes, the transformation? Can you see what God will do? Can you see the creative ideas? Can you see yourself fruitful? Can you see yourself healed? Can you see the future? Can you see the shift? Can you cast the anchor? Can you grab it and cast it in to the future? Say this: "In a year, I will look much better than I do right now." Our hope is founded on the Word of God. It is not a utopia or an ideal; rather, it is hope in a living God. Jesus said, "Upon this rock, I will build My Church, and the gates of Hades will not prevail against it." The devil may come, hell may roar, and the world and the demons may blow, but your ship will not sink, because you are anchored to the Rock.

Conclusion

The Word of God teaches us that we will know the truth, and this truth will set us free. This chapter has revealed a fundamental truth for Christians to remain and live in victory, even in times of crisis. The mystery of the helmet of salvation that Paul wrote about in his letter to the Ephesians is a truth that will make the difference in our lives. It is not the same to try to overcome a crisis, fighting against all the negative thoughts the enemy constantly sends us by every means available—radio, television, newspapers, politicians, economists, neighbors, family members, and more—as it is to have the helmet of salvation in Christ protecting our thoughts. The mind is the battlefield, and Satan knows that well. An unbalanced mind cannot focus correctly. The helmet of hope is a grip for our minds, for us to hold on to the promises of salvation written in the Bible. Christ in me, the hope of glory!

Christians should be optimistic by nature because they have received the revelation that their salvation comes from Jesus, not from the world or its prosperity. If we love God and are aligned to His will and purpose, our salvation will be secured. Hope is also an exceedingly strong counsel, an anchor for our soul when the sea of this world is being stirred. In times of crisis let us run to our hope, which is Jesus Christ, grabbing on to His promises and His presence in the altar of worship. Let us cover our mind with the helmet of hope, so that the darts of fire from the enemy will not contaminate our thoughts or make us think about defeat. Jesus has secured the victory because God swore it by Himself.

Review:

- The armor that Paul describes offers no protection to the back because we are not supposed to give our back to the enemy, but rather confront him face to face. We cannot run, but instead must face the enemy with hope and boldness in any crisis in our life.

- The roman helmet was made of leather, and lined with metal strips, and was used to protect the head and parts of the neck.

- Protecting the head is paramount, because it is there that the mind is and that thoughts dwell. They lead the individual to optimism or pessimism.

- In times of crisis, people's greatest problem is their mind. The enemy attacks their thoughts to lead them to desperation and death.

- Hope is a mental expectation of something good. We must protect it with the helmet of salvation.

- Faith comes by hearing the Word of God, and it travels to the heart by the confession of our mouths.

- Our hope is in Christ, the author and finisher of our faith.

- God's thoughts for us are of peace and of a successful future. We need to have the mind of Christ.

- All things work together for those who love God. This promise is fulfilled under the conditions of loving God and being aligned with His purpose.

- We put on the helmet of hope with a prayer of confession of the truths we learned today.

- The two unchanging things that give us security in the promises of God are His Word and His oath.

- Hope is our grip on salvation in order to escape our enemies and to stand against bad news so that they are unable to reach us. It is a powerful counsel to anchor to the strong Rock that is Jesus Christ.

- Hope is a hidden refuge in Christ. Christ in you is the hope of glory! He is the hope of salvation, deliverance, provision, prosperity, health, and creativity that enables you to deal with crisis and emerge from it as a genuine conqueror.

❧ ❧ ❧

CHAPTER X

How to Respond to a Crisis

❧ ❧ ❧

I f we must experience a crisis or shaking, we must do so correctly. We need to build a solid foundation over the Word of God. Jesus said that we must hear His Word and obey it, and this chapter goes along that line. The question is not, "What should we do?" but rather, "How should we walk?" Who we are is more important than what we do, and He says we must walk in holiness and godliness.

"17Therefore 'Come out from among them and be separate, says the Lord. Do not touch what is unclean, and I will receive you.' 18'I will be a Father to you, and you shall be My sons and daughters,' says the LORD Almighty." 2 Corinthians 6:17, 18

God left promises in the Bible, and their fulfillment depends on certain conditions which include separation from the world and the refusal to touch unclean things. There are many ways to touch unclean things: through our thoughts, eyes, ears (watching "dirty" or horror shows or movies, reading inappropriate magazines, or saying bad words, with our hands, our feet, and the places we go. Do not expose yourself to impurity or run towards evil.

࿊࿊࿊

Sooner or later, the filth in our mind comes out through our mouth and manifests in our actions.

࿊࿊࿊

Ask yourself today, "Am I touching something dirty or worldly? Am I exposing myself to things that will stain or contaminate my spirit?" If your heart is pure, you will have a pure life; but, if it is impure, that will be reflected in your life. This is a spiritual law that governs mankind.

What will happen if we keep His commands?

"18'I will be a Father to you, and you shall be My sons and daughters,' says the LORD Almighty." 2 Corinthians 6:18

Paul connects this and says:

"1Therefore, having these promises, beloved, let us cleanse ourselves from all filthiness of the flesh and spirit, perfecting holiness in the fear of God." 2 Corinthians 7:1

There are certain things that God does for us, but there are others we must do ourselves. There are parts of holiness that only God can complete, but there are others that we must rid ourselves of in order to be holy.

- **Filthiness of the flesh:** Sexual immorality, fornication, adultery, lasciviousness, drunkenness, anger, etcetera.

- **Filthiness of the spirit:** Every form of contact with the occult. Many are unaware that they are involved in the occult. (horoscopes, cursed objects, etcetera)

What should we expect?

In the Scriptures, we can see that holiness is tied to the

coming of the Lord. When the Church stops expecting His coming, which serves as the strongest motivation, they then lose sight of the standards of holiness found in the New Testament.

"³And everyone who has this hope in Him purifies himself, just as He is pure." 1 John 3:3

You might say that you believe in His second coming, but I would look for evidence of that in your life, i.e., holiness and purification. Paul states that the responsibility is on us and establishes a standard of holiness.

"¹²looking for and hastening the coming of the day of God..."
2 Peter 3:12

It is not enough to expect Jesus' coming in His glory and majesty. We must also quicken it by proclaiming the Gospel and working for every person to have a chance to hear His voice and be saved.

"¹⁴And this gospel of the kingdom will be preached in all the world as a witness to all the nations, and then the end will come."
Matthew 24:14

This is the most important sign, for the Gospel to be preached in the whole world. We are responsible to preach it. If we don't, we are slowing down His coming.

"⁷Let us be glad and rejoice and give Him glory, for the marriage of the Lamb has come, and His wife has made herself ready."
Revelations 19:7

The marriage of the Lamb cannot take place if the bride is not prepared. Thus, the state of the Church affects the coming of the Lord. If she is not prepared, her husband cannot come for her.

"8And to her it was granted to be arrayed in fine linen, clean and bright, for the fine linen is the righteous acts of the saints." *Revelations 19:8*

The wedding dress is of fine linen which represents the good works we must do.

Here we find the foundation of what we should do in the face of global shakings or personal crises.

Five principles on how to respond to crisis

1. Align ourselves with the will of God

God has clearly revealed to us His purpose. He has never changed it, and He works consistently.

"10Your kingdom come. Your will be done on earth as it is in heaven." *Matthew 6:10*

God's main goal is for His Kingdom to come to Earth, and the only way we can align ourselves with His will is by means of finding His purpose. Only when everything we do is led towards establishing His Kingdom can we say that we are aligned with His purpose.

"33But seek first the kingdom of God and His righteousness and all these things shall be added to you." *Matthew 6:33*

The Kingdom must be sought first, not in second or third place, because it is the only thing that cannot be shaken. It is the only unmoving rock for the Kingdom is Jesus. The only realistic solution to the problems of the world is establishing the Kingdom of God.

Illustration: A practical expression of my commitment to the Kingdom of God is that my preaching and teachings are touching millions of people throughout the world through radio, television, videos, and books. Perhaps you are not called to do the same things as I, but you must still find a way to expand the Kingdom of God. It is not about seeking the Kingdom when it is convenient to you; rather, you must place your priorities in order. Only then will the promise of all things being added be fulfilled. When you place God anywhere but in first place, then every step you take will separate you from His purpose. That, in turn, separates you from your abundance in Christ, as was the case with Jonas.

2. Cultivate perseverance

Three words are found in Scripture that seem to be somewhat similar but which have completely different meanings. They are patience, longsuffering, and perseverance. Now, let us define each one.

- **Patience:** It is translated from the Greek *hupomone*, and means the ability to withstand trials, to be under heavy pressure and persecution, for a long period of time, without becoming discouraged. A simpler definition is that patience is the ability to withstand affliction, problems, or crises, with a calm attitude and without becoming desperate.

- **Longsuffering:** It is the ability to deal with difficult people while keeping one's composure and not losing one's temper.

- **Perseverance:**

  ✓ To remain or take up a position and not move; the power to remain unmoving.

  ✓ Persist, insist, or continue until the objective is completed. This definition is more aggressive because it no longer deals with remaining in one place, but about moving constantly, with a relentless attitude until achieving victory.

  ✓ Claim the blessing through prayer, with courage and without shame.

Perseverance is not simply to suffer with a long face, but to face fear with courage and joy, until we find what we seek. Perseverance is active. In turn, patience is passive as it is to wait. It is far more difficult than simply making things happen. It demands holding on until God takes the initiative.

❧❧❧

Certain blessings only come through patience.

❧❧❧

"12that you do not become sluggish, but imitate those who through faith and patience inherit the promises."
Hebrews 6:12

Some people say that, to reach the fulfillment of God's promises, the only thing we need is faith, but this is not true. We also need patience. God has given countless people a prophetic word concerning their life, ministry, business, etc. Many of them are in a difficult and crucial time of their lives and they say, "What happened to the promises God gave me? Why have they not been fulfilled?" If you are in this category, I remind you that you must continue to wait patiently, because God will complete everything He promised. Observe how Abraham obtained his promise:

"15And so, after he had patiently endured, he obtained the promise." Hebrews 6:15

Patience is part of the condition to be launched by God. At some point, we need to exercise it, especially when He is forming our character to lead us to serve in the ministry and His Kingdom. The teacher is the one who establishes the agenda for the pupil. He decides when the student is ready to practice what he has learned.

Perseverance is to refuse to give up, despite failing time and time again. It is the ability to get back up and continue. Perseverance is to insist, to keep going until God gives us the breakthrough. Perseverance is a persistent, imprudent, daring, bold, intrepid, and shameless diligence. A persistent person is determined, firm, and constant. They resist and challenge all obstacles in their path.

How do we persevere until the end?

"[12]And because lawlessness will abound, the love of many will grow cold." Matthew 24:12

The word *lawlessness* means to live without law. In Matthew, we read that the love of any Christian growing cold is related to lawlessness. Sometimes, we think that walking in love requires no law, discipline, or correction. On the contrary, God corrects us because He loves us.

"[13]But he who endures to the end shall be saved." Matthew 24:13

We need to persevere and fight to the end, despite problems and circumstances. We must face the opposition, and if we fail, we must get back up. There are people who failed in their marriages, in their businesses, in their university studies, or in rearing their children, and believe that their lives have no meaning. I want to encourage you and tell you to keep going, to persevere. Suicide is not the answer. Giving up is not the way out. In these times of crisis, we must keep going despite everything that has happened. The grace of God will come over us and help us in this journey until the coming of the Lord.

How do we develop perseverance?

"³And not only that, but we also glory in tribulations, knowing that tribulation produces perseverance." Romans 5:3

Here we learn what we must do when we encounter tribulations. The secret is to glory in the midst of them. Why is it important to glory during tribulations?

• Tribulation produces perseverance and patience. The only way to develop patience is in a trial. Therefore, do not complain because of them but rather give thanks to the Lord.

• Perseverance produces proven character.

Tribulation is the only thing that produces perseverance; and if we persevere, our character will pass the test. It is crucial to understand that God cannot trust us with important things in His Kingdom if our character has not been tested. Thus, do not complain or murmur for what happens to you. Instead, praise Him and worship Him and continue seeking His Kingdom.

Patience and perseverance are tokens of strength, not of weakness. One of the points described in the letter to the Hebrews is that many people were backsliding after having confessed Jesus as Lord and Savior. The writer warns us about what happens to Christians who were called and filled with the Holy Spirit but decided to turn back because of the problems, persecutions, and tribulations they found on the way.

"35Therefore do not cast away your confidence, which has great reward. 36For you have need of endurance, so that after you have done the will of God, you may receive the promise." Hebrews 10:35, 36

If you do the will of God, you should receive the promise. What do you need to have to receive it? We need perseverance, patience, and the passion to remain until the end, i.e., until the will of God is completed and He keeps His promise. Perseverance is paramount.

What is God's promise?

"1Therefore we also, since we are surrounded by so great a cloud of witnesses, let us lay aside every weight, and the sin which so easily ensnares us, and let us run with endurance the race that is set before us, 2looking unto Jesus, the author and finisher of our faith, who for the joy that was set before Him endured the cross, despising the shame, and has sat down at the right hand of the throne of God." Hebrews 12:1, 2

A cloud of witnesses surrounds us. This race is about endurance not speed but about and it requires much perseverance to finish it. We need to finish the race and fulfill God's will for our lives.

To develop perseverance and receive the promise, we must do the following:

• Make a commitment before Jesus Christ, with all our heart, and with no compromise.

"²³When he came and had seen the grace of God, he was glad, and encouraged them all that with purpose of heart they should continue with the Lord." Acts 11:23

Regardless of whether your friends or family left you or if you lost your house and job, you must learn that after making the commitment, you must remain in the will of God.

- **Tribulations develop perseverance.**

"²²strengthening the souls of the disciples, exhorting them to continue in the faith, and saying, 'We must, through many tribulations, enter the kingdom of God.'"
Acts 14:22

Tribulation is the way to enter God's Kingdom. We will experience pressure in all areas of our lives because God is preparing us to establish His Kingdom on Earth. We must warn people about this truth. It is unfair to tell new believers that when they come to Jesus they will have no more problems or ever suffer again. It does not work that way. They are going to have problems, perhaps more than ever. Likewise, however, more than ever before, God will be by their side and give them the victory.

- **Keep our eyes on the Invisible.**

"²⁷By faith he forsook Egypt, not fearing the wrath of the king; for he endured as seeing Him who is invisible."
Hebrews 11:27

What does it mean to keep our eyes on the Invisible? What is the ability that allows us to see the Invisible? The answer is faith, the conviction of things unseen. If you and I are going to persevere, we need to see an invisible world that is more real than the visible; otherwise, we will not persevere.

* **Continue until the end. Refuse to give up.**

One of the enemy's biggest traps is to tell you to give up, that you are a failure, and that it would be better if you just stopped. The devil is a liar. David, Peter, and many other great man of the Bible fell tremendously. However, they did not give up and instead persevered until the end.

* **Remember the promise that awaits us.**

There are rewards that many people will receive on Earth, but many others will be given in Heaven.

"⁸Finally, there is laid up for me the crown of righteousness, which the Lord, the righteous Judge, will give to me on that Day, and not to me only but also to all who have loved His appearing." 2 Timothy 4:8

There are crowns of gold, bronze, and many other metals that the Lord has prepared for us. Days are coming where our perseverance and patience will be tested. We have received a testimony in our spirit that tells us that the situation will not be easy; persecution and problems will come. However, we will remain firm, unwavering, and waiting for Jesus to give us the victory. If other men were able to fulfill their purpose, why shouldn't we be able to fulfill ours?

- **We must ask God to give us His grace to persevere until the end.**

"12 ...the signs of an apostle were accomplished among you with all perseverance, in signs and wonders and mighty deeds." 2 Corinthians 12:12

We cannot stop because perseverance is connected with destiny. This is the only way to reach a glorious future. If we are going to respond to crisis correctly, we will only do so by asking God for His grace to remain firm. This is how we will continue until we finish the work He has placed in our hands. If we fail, let us get back up, ask God for forgiveness, and strive until the end. If we feel powerless, let us ask for His grace to strengthen us. Let us wait with patience, praising Him, and thanking Him. In doing this, we know that the testing of our faith produces patience, that patience yields a proven character, that a proven character generates hope; and it is that hope which will give us the victory by means of Jesus Christ, who takes us from glory to glory.

3. Wait on God

Waiting is a word that has been underappreciated in the Church of Christ, but it is an essential condition to prepare us for the coming of the Lord.

"28So Christ was offered once to bear the sins of many. To those who eagerly wait for Him He will appear a second time, apart from sin, for salvation." Hebrews 9:28

We need to be expectant for the coming of the Lord.

"4For since the beginning of the world men have not heard nor perceived by the ear, nor has the eye seen any God besides You, who acts for the one who waits for Him." Isaiah 64:4

This describes one of God's unique traits. He works in favor of those who wait on Him.

"4I must work the works of Him who sent Me while it is day; the night is coming when no one can work." John 9:4

Let us do His will while it is still day. However, waiting does not mean to sit down and do nothing. This is an active wait, while doing the will of God. This way, we will be ready when what was promised to us finally arrives. Waiting is a test that God places in the path of every servant He wants to use.

Examples of men who waited on God:

- Abraham waited 25 years for what God had promised him, that is, his son Isaac.

- Joseph suffered and waited for thirty years to see his family again and be redeemed from the evil done to him by his brothers.

"17He sent a man before them—Joseph—who was sold as a slave. 18They hurt his feet with fetters, he was laid in irons. 19Until the time that his word came to pass, the word of the LORD tested him." Psalms 105:17-19

- Moses had to wait in the desert for forty years before returning to Egypt and delivering the people of God.

- David waited fifteen years to be anointed as king of Israel.

God allowed these men to undergo these circumstances and times of waiting for one reason, to develop their patience and perseverance. You cannot skip the test and enter directly into the promises of God. If you are in the middle of a trial, do not give up. Hold on and persevere until the end. Waiting teaches us to depend more and more on God. We cannot make it happen on our own strength, nor do we know when our desire will be fulfilled or God's promise will come. We can only depend on Him and wait with joy.

4. Ask God for the boldness to overcome fear

"73The oath which He swore to our father Abraham: 74To grant us that we, being delivered from the hand of our enemies, might serve Him without fear, 75In holiness and righteousness before Him all the days of our life." Luke 1:73-75

If God tells us to seek His Kingdom and righteousness, we cannot be afraid of tomorrow, of the obstacles that the enemy might try to put in our path, or of the crisis that is shaking this world. The word of God is crystal-clear in regards to the protection He gives us. There is no place for fear in our lives if the love of God is in our heart.

"³Surely He shall deliver you from the snare of the fowler and from the perilous pestilence. ⁴He shall cover you with His feathers, and under His wings you shall take refuge; His truth shall be your shield and buckler. ⁵You shall not be afraid of the terror by night, nor of the arrow that flies by day, ⁶nor of the pestilence that walks in darkness, nor of the destruction that lays waste at noonday. ⁷A thousand may fall at your side, and ten thousand at your right hand; but it shall not come near you." Psalms 91:3-7

If the enemy has attacked your life with fear then renounce that spirit. Strengthen yourself in the power of your God, fight the good fight of faith, and work towards eternal life.

5. **Develop a positive attitude and expectancy for the future.**

Most people are born and raised with pessimism and thus fight against hopelessness, depression, and many other negative feelings. Paul tells us many problems are to come, yet he affirms his hope in God's promises.

Who is more than a conqueror?

"³⁷Yet in all these things we are more than conquerors through Him who loved us." Romans 8:37

A person is more than a conqueror when he faces a problem, overcomes it, and when he emerges from it, he does so with more virtues than when he went in. If we believe that God is almighty, then it is very foolish to think that the devil can defeat Him. Nevertheless, at times we are invaded by doubt.

"⁷He who overcomes shall inherit all things, and I will be his God and he shall be My son." Revelations 21:7

There is not one promise found in the New Testament destined for deserters, for those who are left behind, for the ones who become discouraged, for the ones who fell asleep, or for the ones who allowed themselves to be defeated. I only found promises, and I found them in abundance, for those who overcome, who persevere, who remain, who vigil, and who take their blessings by force. We have no other option. All of us can overcome, but the choice is ours.

Review:

• God's promises have certain conditions, i.e., coming out of the crowd, separating ourselves, and refusing to touch the world.

• We must separate ourselves from the things of the world to develop holiness in our lives.

* There is contamination of the flesh, through the senses, and contamination of the spirit, by means of practicing the occult.

* We can hasten the coming of Christ by preaching the Gospel.

* The five practical principles to hear the Word of God and obey it are aligning ourselves with the purpose of God, cultivating perseverance, waiting on God, asking Him for boldness to overcome fear, and developing a positive attitude and expectation for the future.

* A conqueror is a person who faces a problem, overcomes it, and when he does so, he comes out of it with more virtues than when he first encountered in.

* When we confront evil with good, we become His mouthpiece that speaks salvation and truth.

BIBLIOGRAPHY

᳅᳅᳅

Expanded Edition the Amplified Bible. Zondervan Bible Publishers, 1987 - Lockman Foundation, USA. ISBN: 0-31095168-2

Real Academia Española, *Diccionario de la Lengua Española,* http://www.rae.es/.

Reina-Valera 1960, Copyright © 1960 Sociedades Bíblicas en América Latina; Copyright © renovado 1988, Sociedades Bíblicas Unidas.

Strong, James. *LL.D, S.T.D.* Nueva Concordancia Strong Exhaustiva. *Nashville, TN–Miami, FL: Editorial Caribe, Inc./División Thomas Nelson Publishers,* 2002. ISBN: 0-89922-382-6.

The Tormont Webster's Illustrated Encyclopedic Dictionary. ©1990 Tormont Publications.

Vine, W.E. *Vine: diccionario expositivo de palabras del antiguo testamento y del nuevo testamento exhaustivo.* Nashville, TN: Editorial Caribe, Inc./División de Thomas Nelson, Inc., 1999. ISBN: 0-89922-495-4.

Ward, Lock A. *Nuevo Diccionario de la Biblia.* Editorial Unilit: Miami, Florida, 1999. ISBN: 0-7899-0217-6

Holy Bible, NIV. 1973, 1978, 1984 International Bible Society.